BOOK 1 *of* THE YELLOW HOUSE SERIES

the

yellow house

Foundations

An Autobiography of Hope

Ronald Sparks

ILLUMIFY
MEDIA.COM

The Yellow House

Copyright © 2026 by Ronald Sparks

Published by
Illumify Media Global
www.IllumifyMedia.com
"Let's bring your book to life!"

Library of Congress Control Number:

Paperback ISBN: 978-1-970582-03-1

Cover design by Debbie Lewis

Printed in the United States of America

This book is dedicated to my family and friends who each had a part, large or small, in helping lay and shape my foundation as I grew up, especially Mom. She's the one I loved most and who showed me the most love when I was growing up. Thanks, Mom.

Contents

Prologue

WHILE GROWING UP AS KIDS in Chillicothe, Ohio, we referred to some of our homes by color, at least after we had
moved away. As a teenager, my siblings and I began to refer
to our homes by street name. Not the specific address, just
the street name. I have no idea why, other than possibly
because many of them were the same color or because,
as we aged, there was a bit more sophistication to a street
name than house color. However, the first two homes I remember living in we identified by color.

In the case of the house we lived in where I had my
first memories, it was called the yellow house. For what
it's worth, the yellow house was on East Second Street in
Chillicothe, Ohio. Yes, the "east end" of town—shout-outs
to all my east-end friends who may read this book.

My sister Donna shared that we lived in three other
houses before we moved to the yellow house. She didn't

remember the color of each house, just the street name. Maybe it's that sophistication theory again.

Donna said I was born and first lived on Hirn Street. Then we moved to Fairview Street, then again to Mulberry Street. However, I have no memories of those houses, just a couple of stories my siblings shared with me growing up. Think about it for a moment. I lived in four different houses before turning age five.

So, my first memories are from when we lived in the yellow house. They were profound, life-shaping memories that set some of the foundation for my life.

Before reading any further, please know there are some chapters that include actions that are incredibly embarrassing for me. I'm not proud of those things. I wish I could go back in time and make better choices, but I can't. It's part of my story now, and I ask you to please not judge me based on the darker parts of my life.

1

The Yellow House . . . Of Hate

ONE OF THE EARLIEST AND most significant first memory was my fifth birthday, in July 1975. My dad, Don, told my mom, Nancy, he wanted to take me somewhere special for my birthday.

Turning five is a big deal.

Mind you, I was the youngest of six of Dad's children and five Dad and Mom had together. I have four older sisters and one older brother. This meant I was also the second son, with my brother, Donnie, being the first son.

So, for Dad to want to take me, just me, somewhere special for my fifth birthday was wonderful in my early and innocent memory.

I loved to play outside as a kid, regardless of how hot, cold, wet, dry, muddy it was, or whatever the conditions were. It was quite the ordeal for Mom to drag me inside and attempt to get me all cleaned up for this special trip.

Knowing I would take forever, Mom ushered my tiny butt into the bathtub and began scrubbing away.

"We have to hurry up, honey. Your daddy is waiting."

Mom always called me honey. She repeated herself once I was out of the tub and as she helped me put on my very best clothes, which I seem to recall were a pair of slim-sized slacks, a long-sleeve shirt, and a light, sport-type jacket, all from Goodwill. I wasn't allowed to wear my cutoff jean shorts, which in the summer was pretty much all I wore.

"Mommy, where's Daddy taking me?"

There was no eye contact or certainty in her voice, either perhaps not truly knowing where he was taking me or suspecting it was someplace she wouldn't approve.

"I'm not sure, honey. It's a surprise."

I'll never know for sure, but in hindsight, I suspect she was suspicious.

I got in the car with Dad as Mom waved good-bye from the doorway. I was all clean for the special day, fidgeting a bit, and full of excitement.

"Daddy, where are we going?"

He was also cleaned up and dressed to impress with at least one or two extra splashes of Avon Musk cologne.

"We'll be there in a little while."

I must have asked at least a half dozen more times, and his response was always the same.

The drive seemed long. I remembered the uncertainty in Mom's voice from earlier. My excitement dampened.

As we neared our destination, in a deep, stern voice, with serious eyes glaring at me, and me then nervously looking back at him, it started.

"Do not tell Mommy where we went. If you do, you're gonna get a spanking."

It didn't make any sense to me. Why couldn't I share with Mom this exciting surprise?

We pulled into a dirt driveway of a house and parked.

I knew we weren't going to a park, a restaurant, or anywhere considered worthy of a surprise label.

I was also sure this was someplace Mom would not approve, and now I knew why she had uncertainty in her voice.

"Get out of the car and come with me."

I obeyed. What else was I going to do? My stomach began to ache from the nervousness. I had a weak stomach at that age anyway.

Dad knocked on the door but then walked right in. Why didn't he wait for someone to answer? Did he know them?

He did know them, because once inside, some woman came out of the kitchen and gave Dad a kiss, on the lips.

My stomach ached and turned even more at the sight. It was then, at that very moment, I learned how to hate.

As the hate welled up inside me, I wasn't thinking I just got cheated out of a birthday surprise. I was thinking about Mom. How could he do this to her? She was such a beautiful woman, inside and out.

This other woman, who didn't say her name or acknowledge me in any way, was not beautiful. She was ugly. She was not my mom. I hated her as much as I hated Dad at that moment. Two times the hate in as many minutes.

Dad glanced at me.

"Remember what I told you. Stay here and play. I'll be in the back."

There was another kid there, presumably this lady's kid, who was about my age. Dad didn't acknowledge him, just like this woman didn't acknowledge me. The kid was filthy. The house was filthy.

Sure, there were times when I was filthy, and our house wasn't always the best kept with five kids running around, but today I was clean and didn't want to be around a filthy kid in a filthy house.

I hated this kid. I hated this house I was in. Two more bouts of hate, just like that.

I don't remember exactly how long Dad was "in the back" with this woman, but it was way longer than I wanted to be there. We eventually left, got in the car, and drove straight home. I couldn't say anything to Dad, and he didn't say anything until we pulled up to our house. When he did say something, there was no remorse in his voice.

"Tell Mommy we went to Dairy Queen and the park."

I did so out of fear, fear of the spanking he promised because Dad was a big dude and could be intimidating. So, I obeyed and never mentioned it until I was an even more hate-filled teenager trying to get back at him.

Here's a rather pathetic correlation to this story. My sister Donna told me I was born in Circleville, Ohio, at Berger Hospital. When Mom was pregnant with me, Dad left for days, off cheating with other women. Mom knew this, and rather than be left sitting at home, she wanted to be with her family. She made Dad take her and my siblings to her parents' house. We were there when she went into labor. He was cheating and not there when I was born. Then with my first real memory of him, he was cheating again.

As I grew up, I had so many questions. Why did Dad cheat on Mom? He was thirty-four at the time, and Mom was thirty-one. They had been married fourteen years at this point. Again, Mom was so beautiful and had the sweetest soul and most gentle nature.

Why did she tolerate it? Perhaps out of fear of being abandoned? She was sixteen when they got married. She only had an elementary school education. I'm sure she didn't know what to do.

Why did Dad use me in his plan to cheat? He could have come up with some other excuse to get away and cheat.

Was this kid my half-brother?

Whatever happened to this woman?

Was she a home wrecker multiple times over, with multiple men?

Was she carrying sexually transmitted diseases that could pass to Dad and then on to Mom?

What did Mom do to deserve this?

How could Dad be so selfish and cruel?

Dad did other things, or sometimes nothing, over the years we lived in the yellow house. They only deepened my hatred of him. Here are a few.

One night, he came home from somewhere after being gone for a long time, even overnight. It was the same summer after my fifth birthday. Mom told him to go out to the backyard, as she wanted to talk with him. She was angry.

My curiosity got the best of me, so I watched and listened through the kitchen window.

She was shaking, and her voice cracked. "If you ever do that again, I'm going to . . ." And she smacked him across the face. A burning cigarette flew out of his mouth and onto the ground.

I'm assuming it was his cheating again because I had never seen Mom this angry. Probably the same woman he was with when he dragged me into his mess. I could tell he had hurt her deeply. So much she became violent. I hated Dad for that.

Mom's sister, Aunt Rosie, and her husband, Uncle Tom, also lived in Circleville. I loved it when we visited them because I loved them and my cousins, Karen, Chrissy, Angie, Tommy, and Patricia. Tommy and I ran around all over the place getting into mischief. He was just a little younger than me, so we had fun hanging out together.

When I was around six, Dad took us up there. He came in for a little bit and visited with the rest of us. We usually were all in the same room at first, sharing greetings and doing the quick catching up before the kids would break away to go play.

Dad said he was going to run to the store to grab a few things. Seems normal, right, maybe picking up some beers or some snacks? Well, he didn't return for two days.

We had no idea where he was. Uncle Tom and Aunt Rosie accommodated us because they were wonderful people. However, Mom was embarrassed. She didn't seem fearful, though, and in hindsight, I thought it was odd. If my wife, Kahala, were to unexpectedly disappear for two days, I would absolutely fear the worst.

Mom kept making excuses for Dad, hiding her embarrassment, but I could tell she was upset. He was at it again. Likely off with another woman, smoking, drinking, and doing pills. As much fun as I had at Uncle Tom and Aunt Rosie's house, I didn't like seeing Mom embarrassed and hurt. I hated Dad for that.

For birthdays and at Christmas, Dad always wrapped up a girl's baby doll, claiming it was just a toy, such as a new Hot Wheels car or something most boys like. As a kid, I was always excited about opening any wrapped gift, so I always opened it. It never failed when I opened these gifts, there was a girl's baby doll of some sort inside. A barbie doll or whatever.

Now, Dad was known to be a prankster, but why would he repeatedly do this to his youngest son, especially after I signaled the first time that I didn't like it? After having four girls, was he content with my older brother being the only boy he needed and wished I was a girl?

I was a rambunctious little boy, all boy and an adventurous spirit, for that matter. Yes, I had a gentle-natured side to me as well, a little introverted and quiet at times, with my blond hair and blue eyes, but I didn't have a feminine nature about me. So why force this upon me? He only did this to me. I never understood why. I didn't like it, and I hated Dad for that.

There were other things.

Why didn't Dad figure out a way to get rid of all the water bugs and cockroaches that came out like a regiment across the kitchen floor at night?

When I went to get a drink of water at night, I had to turn Dad's cowboy boots upside down to shake the bugs out of there first. Then I put them on and clamped through the kitchen, smashing them. It was disgusting.

Why didn't Dad buy another box fan for the room my brother Donnie and I had to share? They were less than ten dollars in the mid to late '70s.

Summers in the Scioto River valley were brutally hot and humid. I was forced to sneak into the girls' room and steal the box fan they had, at least for a little while or until they woke up sweating and came to take it back. I had a bike lock and eventually locked it to the bed so they couldn't take it back. Yeah, fun times that could have been fixed by a ten-dollar second fan.

Why were we always running out of food, especially the last week of the month?

Why did I have to be the one to go ask Grandpa Sparks, who lived next door to us, if we could borrow food from the Cedar Haven Rest Home he ran or borrow money for food? Dad wrote notes and sent me with the notes to ask.

Why was it always me? Perhaps because I was the youngest and Grandpa Sparks had pity on me.

Why didn't Dad pay our utilities so they wouldn't get shut off all the time?

We often relied on space heaters in the winter, and there was no hot water for bath time because the gas was shut off. We had to boil hot water on an electric stove. Winters in Ohio were brutally cold just like the summers were brutally hot.

Why did Dad leave *Playboy*, *Hustler*, and a variety of other pornographic magazines lying around the house where they could be found? Didn't he know the damage this type of material can cause in the minds of young boys?

Why did he spend money on that crap anyway, especially when we were always borrowing food or money to get food?

Why didn't Dad pay the rent on time?

Wasn't he also tired of the threat of eviction and moving, or did he just not care?

Eventually, we would get evicted from the yellow house. The landlord was our next-door neighbor. They had kids, too, and we played with them. It was embarrassing when their dad evicted us. It was also upsetting that we wouldn't live next door to Grandpa Sparks any longer. I hated Dad for this and all the other things I just mentioned.

Yes, some of the things are not a big deal, but nonetheless, they are fuel to a fire of hatred that had built up. And they would also later influence how I handled marriage, parenting, adult responsibilities, and even the minute detail of running my ceiling fan all night long, even in the dead of winter, since I didn't have a fan most of the time growing up.

2
The Yellow House . . . Of Love

I WANT YOU TO KNOW Dad was not a bad person 100 percent of the time. He did have a few good moments, which I'm sure my siblings can attest to as well.

He bought Donnie and me Red Ryder BB guns for Christmas one year. He also bought us Huffy Pro Thunder bikes for summer another year. He bought my sisters marijuana smoking kits. I know, right?! Yeah, they loved them.

I often wondered if material things were his way of trying to make up for all the bad things he did. However, as a poor kid, these things were like winning the lottery. I have no idea where he got the money for these things, but I suspect it wasn't legal.

We also went fishing from time to time. Dad managed a pay lake at one point. You basically paid to fish there, almost guaranteeing a catch, as the lakes were stocked full of fish.

If not fishing there, we fished at Northfolk Creek nearby where Dad's sister, Aunt Maxine, and her husband, Uncle Charlie, lived.

Dad loved to fish, and we kids loved to fish as well. This wasn't a material thing but rather a precious moment of family time I longed for as a child. Fishing with Dad was my most positive childhood experience. I still hold on to those memories today, wishing we could fish together just once more.

Dad had a couple of jobs before basically retiring full-time on workers' compensation checks. He was a truck driver for a little while, and I went on a trip or two with him. There's nothing like riding in a semi-truck at a young age. These were the bright spots or little bits of love that occasionally flared amid the hate.

My love for others also stood out amid the hate, and there were a few people I loved dearly as a child. I'm sure there are many ways you can tell how much you love someone. For me, when I felt at a very young age the pain Mom was feeling, I knew I had a deep love for her.

I loved Mom something fierce and absolutely clung to her. I could be outside for five minutes, and if I came back inside and didn't see her, I asked, "Where's Mom?"

If she heard me, which was likely because she was almost always around, I would hear her soft, loving voice that provided a sense of security for me. "I'm right here, honey."

I asked this question whenever I came home for the rest of her life, even after I had gone away to the United States Marine Corps and come home on leave. Her response was always the same.

Mom was always there for me, protecting me as best she could. She fed my siblings and me as best she could with food stamps or what little money she made working for Grandpa Sparks at Cedar Haven. Dad typically took the welfare check and most of what Mom made in earnings, but she always managed to take care of us, especially when Dad took off for days.

As many little kids did back in the '70s, we often fell asleep somewhere in the living room or near a TV. When that happened, Mom carried me upstairs to my bedroom. Granted, I was skinny as a rail and probably weighed fifty pounds soaking wet, but still, she picked me up and made sure I got to bed. She made me feel safe. I loved Mom for that.

I got chicken pox during the dead of winter one year. Remember, I always wanted to be outside, and it had been snowing endlessly. In fact, it was a snow day from school, and my brother, and all our friends were outside playing in the snow. I begged Mom for hours to let me go outside despite having chicken pox. She eventually caved, wrapped me up like Randy from *A Christmas Story*, and sent me out.

Some may question her parenting for allowing me to go outside with chicken pox. Perhaps she did it to get me out of her hair, or perhaps she did it because she knew how much I loved to be outside, and she wanted me to have fun because she loved me. Either way, the next day, the chicken pox was way worse.

As I whined because the chicken pox itched so bad, her warm hands applying anti-itching cream, I heard that same loving voice, with no condemnation for making a bad choice. "Honey, I told you the chicken pox would get worse, but I hope you had fun yesterday."

I loved Mom for that.

One summer when I was seven years old, I was in the backyard throwing a baseball around with friends. Mom had a parakeet that sat in its cage hanging near the top of our kitchen window. The parakeet's name was Sparky. Pretty original given our last name, right?!

Mom loved that parakeet. She talked to it all the time when she was doing dishes or generally cleaning up the kitchen. I can't remember how she got it. Likely one of Dad's makeup gifts.

Anyway, I threw the baseball toward the house where a friend was standing. He didn't catch it because it was thrown high, and it went right through the top part of the kitchen window, hitting Sparky's cage and knocking the cage to the kitchen floor. Sparky lived, at least for the rest of the day. However, he was found dead in his cage the next morning.

I maintain he died of natural causes, but all my siblings said I killed Sparky. They said he likely had some form of heart attack from the initial shock of the baseball hitting his cage, and he died a slow, painful death overnight.

I told Mom I was sorry. Upset and very sad, she managed to say, "It's okay, honey. It was an accident."

It made me sad to see her so sad. I suppose she could have punished me any number of ways, but she didn't. She showed mercy and forgiveness. I loved Mom for that.

Mom showed countless other acts of love over my life. I loved her the most growing up. I miss her dearly.

I also loved Grandma Sparks. She lived right next door to us when we were in the yellow house. When Mom did work at Cedar Haven, and before I was in kindergarten, she carried me, half-asleep, over to Grandma's house in the wee hours of the morning. Mom had to be at Cedar Haven early, along with Grandpa Sparks, to start preparing breakfast and other things for the day. Mom would take me inside and lay me beside Grandma, who was typically still in bed.

Grandma Sparks was a bigger lady, so I would snuggle up next to her warmth, in that warm bed, and doze back to full sleep. Eventually, we woke up, her before me, and she always made me some sort of fun breakfast. Pancakes,

French toast, or something that we didn't normally get at home. Throughout the morning and early afternoon, she read to me or allowed me to play around the house like any four-year-old.

Unfortunately, I only have about a year of that memory. Grandma Sparks died shortly after I turned five years old, in August 1975.

During the viewing, as Grandma lay in her casket, Mom took me up to see her. She lifted me up so I could see better. As she was doing so, Mom turned to someone behind us and whispered, "He doesn't understand."

Oh, but I did understand. I didn't know how Grandma died, but I did know we would no longer have snuggle time, her reading to me, or fun breakfasts together. Mostly, I would miss her kind, gentle nature and warm personality.

I loved Grandpa Sparks and felt sad for him after Grandma died. They were married a long time, and I saw the deep love he showed her when she was alive. I still went over to their house after Grandma passed away, and I knew Grandpa was heartbroken.

Grandpa was still always kind, at least to me. Yes, most of the time he saw me, I had a note in my hand asking for food or money. There wasn't a time when he didn't give me something, maybe not exactly what Dad wanted, but something.

Then there was Grandpa and Grandma Hill. They lived in a trailer park on the far eastern side of town. We eventually lived in that same trailer park. We visited them whenever possible, usually on Sundays when other family also visited. They had a lot of grandchildren from Mom and her sisters and brothers.

Grandma had a wooden rocking chair she was always rocking in. She, too, was a bigger lady, and she took up nearly all the space of her rocking chair. However, she let me find a way to squeeze my tiny butt into her rocking chair with her, and we rocked together. She wasn't a gentle woman per se, as she would pat me on the back over and over again rather sternly as I rocked with her in her rocking chair.

Perhaps it was because I was Mom's youngest and one of her younger grandchildren, or perhaps it was because we shared the same birthday, but I was usually the only one she let rock with her. It made me feel special, and I loved her for how much love she showed me.

Grandpa Hill was a drinker, but he was also a gentle-natured man. I believe he suffered reverse tolerance from drinking so much, or he had just killed too many brain cells, because he became drunk after only a few beers.

I was an early riser as a kid, up at the crack of dawn, but I could never be up before Grandpa Hill was awake. Maybe it's because he fell asleep early from drinking, but when I stayed over at their house, I woke up and went into the kitchen and he was there.

Grandpa Hill would always be rolling a Bugler cigarette. His fingers were yellow from smoking those things.

However, it was his pleasure, and it was a cheap pleasure. As I strolled in, I always mumbled, "Good morning, Grandpa."

He would softly say, "Good morning, honey."

Perhaps that's why Mom always called me honey, because Grandpa Hill called her honey when she was growing up.

I would sit there with him in the smoke-filled kitchen and talk for a little while. He always asked if I wanted something to eat. They didn't have much either, and how they were able to keep so many grandchildren overnight was beyond me, but he always found some cereal or something for me to eat.

He may have had his faults, but he was a good man, a wonderful grandfather, and I loved him for how much love he showed me.

You may be wondering about my siblings. Well, at this point in my life, when you're five to ten years old, the youngest of five children, it's kind of like Kevin in *Home Alone*.

I do love my sisters and brother today, of course, but they weren't the ones who necessarily showed me love or how to love at an early age. In fact, I was almost always at war with my sisters.

They pulled my underwear up my butt crack, and I threw knives or sixteen-ounce pop bottles at them. I struck Donna in the back of the head with a pop bottle once. She had just finished torturing me over something else. It was an epic feud.

I do have to share one quick story about Donnie. He was held back in the first grade for missing too much school. He never wanted to go to school in kindergarten or first grade. Since I was just a grade behind him, we were suddenly in first grade together the year after he was held back.

We were at school, and there were at least two groups of first graders who were clustered into a larger room setting. Basically, we were in separate first grade classes, but I could see him not too far away. It was raining hard outside, along with thunder and some loud cracks of lightning. Donnie was afraid of storms.

Well, after a big bolt of lightning struck, he looked over at me, started to cry, and said to his teacher, "I want my brother."

Now, say those words but draw it out in a long, whiney voice. I was so embarrassed I slid down my seat to try to hide. However, I also felt needed and loved by Donnie at that point.

As I learned to love in the yellow house and throughout my life, I expressed it deeply.

Expressing love deeply can lead to an eventual broken heart from a relationship perspective or a shattered heart from a loss perspective. Broken can oftentimes be mended, while shattered is much harder to put back together, if possible at all, and is never the same. I've suffered from both, yet I still choose to love deeply.

3
The Yellow House . . .
Of Prayer

I HAD A NIGHTMARE WHEN I was six years old. I loved to
swim as a kid, either at the city pool in Yoctangee Park or
in the Scioto River.

Yes, in the 1970s kids took off on their bikes, stayed
gone all day long, and sometimes ended up swimming
in a river on a hot summer's day. It was a very real thing
back then and one of the best things about being part of
Generation X.

Back to the dream. I'm swimming somewhere, and
suddenly there are these hideous, sealike creatures with
a jagged fin on their backs and gigantic suction cup of a
mouth filled with razor sharp teeth. They start chasing me.

Do you know how in dreams your movements always seem slow? Well, I'm able at least to swim very slowly to shore, thinking I can then run away. However, when I begin to run, I'm also not running very fast.

To my surprise, the creatures come out of the water too. They have legs like humans, and they can swim and run much faster than I'm running.

They catch and throw me to the ground. They attach their suction mouths to me, and their teeth begin to puncture and shred my flesh.

I wake up in a sweat, terrified.

I'm six years old. I'm so scared. I immediately begin praying.

"God, please protect me, please protect me."

I'm not sure who I'm praying to exactly. Just God in general, I suppose, but somehow I know there is a higher power who can make things better.

How did I know to pray to God? My parents weren't Christians. We didn't go to church. I never remember Mom or Dad talking to me about God or Jesus. Dad occasionally turned on Jimmy Swaggart when he was high, perhaps searching for something himself at the time. However, he never professed to be a Christian, and he certainly didn't try to be a Christian.

I went to vacation Bible school at the First United Methodist Church on Main and Brownell streets, but that was when I was eight or nine years old, not when I was six.

Perhaps Grandma Sparks talked to me about God? I don't remember, but I believe she was a Christian. Maybe when I was younger, three or four, she had me pray or talked to me about God? She had Bibles in her house. Maybe she occasionally read them? I'm not sure. At that time in my life, she was the only person I can think of who might have known God.

Could I have instinctively known there is a God? If true, it raises all kinds of questions.

Why in the world would God allow a six-year-old to have such a horrible nightmare? Was I being punished for Dad's sins?

Was I being punished for my own sin? I wasn't the most innocent six-year-old. Did God allow this to happen to get my attention, even at age six?

Well, it did get my attention, and even if it was fear-based attention, I began to pray every night.

"God, please don't let me have any bad dreams tonight."

I prayed that exact prayer every night for the next seven or so years. Occasionally, I threw in a non-selfish prayer for Mom or perhaps for one of my grandparents, but I always started the same way.

"God, please don't let me have any bad dreams tonight."

I would lie flat on my back, clasp my hands together just between my stomach and chest, and say the prayer. Sometimes I said it softly aloud if no one else was there. If Donnie was there in the bedroom, I didn't say it aloud, but rather to myself. I'm not sure why I didn't say it aloud when someone else was there. I guess I didn't want people to know what I was praying about. At one point, Donnie asked me what I was doing.

I never told anyone about that dream until much later in life, and even then, it was only to a couple of people. I never told anyone about my prayers. It was between me and God.

The miracle of it all is that for all those years I prayed, I never had another nightmare or bad dream. God answered my prayers.

I think God knew it was important that He answer my prayers. He knew it was establishing a foundation that would serve me well much later in life. He also knew how terrified I was and didn't want to see me suffer another dream like that.

There are certainly many other memories I have from living at the yellow house. There are some additional bad ones, but there are just as many good ones.

We walked down and back Second Street to go to school at Mt. Logan Elementary, later renamed Hopewell

Elementary. We had a lot of fun moments with friends, even in the blizzard of 1978.

We went trick-or-treating on that same street and on as many side streets as possible, with a pillowcase full of loot. We dressed as a hobo every year because that was the cheapest and easiest costume available.

We built huge snow forts in the First United Methodist Church parking lot after they plowed it following a heavy snow, back when it used to snow like that in Ohio.

I learned to ride a bike for the first time from Donnie and our friend Brent. Training wheels weren't a thing back then. So they put me on the bike, gave me a strong push, and yelled, "Don't hit the telephone pole!"

I hit the telephone pole. I didn't know how to steer since it was my first time on a bike. I was jerking the handlebars left and right, back and forth, but the bike kept moving forward right toward the telephone pole. It bent the front rim of the bike, and it may have bent my head a little too.

Good memories.

I don't want to give the perception I had a horrible childhood. Overall, I didn't. Yes, there were all the things I mentioned in chapter 1 that stirred hate in my heart for Dad. Yes, there was neglect on his part in a variety of ways, but there was no sexual or physical abuse of any kind.

I know there are kids out there who have suffered far worse, especially when those types of abuses are involved. I'm grateful I was never traumatized by that type of abuse. I was a resilient enough kid to still have fun through Dad's neglect, and growing up in the 1970s in a small town in South Central Ohio—the heart of it all, as they say—was pretty cool.

After a good run of living in the yellow house for five years, we were evicted in 1980. It was after I discovered what it was to hate, what it was to love and be loved, and what it meant to pray and have prayers answered. All three of these things have profoundly impacted the rest of my life.

I was turning ten years old as we prepared to move from the yellow house. I was still young, but I was beginning to figure some things out. Some of those things deepened my hate. Other things showed me what a lack of trust and loyalty looked like. I was still too young to have experienced these things, but regardless, they also shaped who I am today.

4
The White House . . . Of Addiction

NOT THAT WHITE HOUSE. THIS one was literally down the street, not even a block from the yellow house. One might think the landlord of the yellow house had known and perhaps warned the landlord of the white house what to expect. I guess not.

The white house had the usual cockroaches and utilities being shut off from time to time. However, there was a bonus. A gigantic rat terrorized us for what seemed like months. The rat made it into my nightly prayers.

"God, please don't let me have any bad dreams tonight. And God, please don't let the rat bite me."

Dad opted just to live with it. Not me. I told Grandpa Sparks, and he set a trap for it. I watched him set what looked like a bear trap, but Grandpa said it was a rat trap.

After a couple of days, the rat got caught in the trap. I heard the strong snap of the trap and the loud screech of the rat. It kept screeching, so I was not going near the thing. I ran down the block to get Grandpa and ask if he could finish it off for us since Dad was gone somewhere.

He came right away and reached under the kitchen stove with his bare hands where the rat had scurried off to. He pulled the trap out. The rat screeched louder since its tail was the only thing caught in the trap. See, it was a bear trap!

Grandpa proceeded to stomp the rat's head in with the heal of his shoe. I never felt so good about seeing an animal die than in that moment. I also witnessed a true badass for the first time in Grandpa Sparks. He was fearless!

Aside from cockroaches and rats, the good thing about moving just down the street was our neighborhood friends were still around. We also hung out with some other kids we sort of knew before.

We ended up playing a lot of football on Brownell Street with kids like Petey, Dewey, and some others. It was tag football, of course, but we took spills on the paved roads and got a scratch or two. More Generation X mayhem.

As I tried to be a kid, I noticed a pattern in Dad's behavior. About every three to four days, he acted different and stayed up all night banging around the house. Him being "up" went on for a day or two.

He ran around the house wearing boxer shorts and a pair of slippers, even in the dead of winter. He had a towel wrapped around his neck to wipe sweat from his head and neck. Yes, in the dead of winter. He always had a tall Tupperware cup full of ice and Pepsi. He also burned through one or two packs of Camel cigarettes.

After a day or two, Dad would start to fall asleep on the couch, sitting up, mind you, with a cigarette hanging from his mouth, ashes an inch long or more hanging from it. The hot ashes would fall onto his big belly, and he'd snap out of it as he brushed them off. On day three, he faded to nothing.

Why did he act this way? Drugs. Percodan to be exact, which today is better known by its active ingredient, oxycodone. The strength of this medication back in the late 1970s and early 1980s was potent.

The label on the pill bottle recommended taking one pill every five to six hours. Dad took five every one to two hours. Maybe he read the label wrong.

I wish.

Dad was addicted to those things, and it took that many pills to keep his high going. He almost always got prescribed a hundred tablets for his back pain. Taking five at a time meant he took them all within a period of twenty-four to thirty-six hours.

The doctors prescribed him a hundred Percodan, and they also prescribed him a hundred Valium. I learned later the Valium helped him sleep since the Percodan made him so high.

However, Dad didn't take the Valium, or at least not all of them. He sold them to make as much money as possible for his next doctor's visit.

A variety of people came to our door to buy Valium. Many of them were friends of my sisters, and as for the others, we often had no clue who they were.

Dad also gave a few of the Percodan and I believe lots of the Valium to our neighbor John, who sometimes drove him to the doctor. Most of the time, we either didn't have a car or it was broken, so our neighbor or others would have to take Dad. I should have included the lack of a car in the list of things I hated.

Here's how it worked.

Day one, Dad goes to the doctor and gets prescribed the pills, usually late morning or early afternoon. He stays high the rest of the day and all day and night the next day.

On the third day, he crashes hard, sleeping the entire day. I don't know, maybe he did take a few Valium to help him sleep. Or maybe he just crashed because he hadn't slept the previous twenty-four to thirty-six hours.

Come day four, he's literally in pain and the cycle begins again to find out who can prescribe another round.

What did that make Mom and all of us kids? Yeah, Mom was a codependent, and as kids we were just stuck in this never-ending cycle with no end in sight.

Day three was kind of nice. Quiet as he slept. No banging around in the middle of the night like on days one and two as he tried to get ice for his Pepsi. He bought bags of ice that melted between the store and getting into our freezer, which caused the ice to clump together. His efforts to get ice included hammering away with an ice pick, which was very loud and annoying.

Days one and two did have nice moments every now and then as well. Dad sometimes took a little of the extra money from Valium sales to buy a Domino's pizza. Man, what a treat. A boy can only eat cheerios with powdered milk and government cheese for so long. Not to complain, and thank you to whatever government assistance program was in place at this time for those items. I would have been even skinnier if they hadn't been there.

So Dad was an addict, Mom was a codependent, and the rest of us were along for the ride. All in all, I hated it. Later in life I asked, "How did the system fail him so bad he became an addict?" I learned to hate the system and what I considered "bad doctors" as well.

Mom told me later in life Dad hurt his back at a young age while in the United States Army. They medically discharged him, and he continued to have back problems long after. So, when I say he had pain on day four, it was true.

Over the course of his lifetime, Dad had thirty-three back surgeries. Thirty-three! He had scars from the top of his back all the way down to his rear. He bragged about it to people when the topic came up, and he often raised up his shirt and showed them the scars, if he was wearing a shirt.

Why in the world did he need thirty-three surgeries? Was there some medical malpractice along the way? It's no wonder he became addicted, right!

I also understand Dad had degenerative disc disease. I'm told I have the same, but I've only had one lower back surgery. I took whatever painkiller they gave me for the first night after surgery and then disposed of the rest.

Donnie doesn't take any painkillers regardless of his pain level. He's too afraid of becoming addicted.

Over time you can get comfortable with the cycle and even participate in it. I occasionally accompanied Dad and Mom to the doctor—that is, if we had a car at the time and it was in working condition.

Here's how it worked.

Dad stops off at a local store and buys a large fruit basket for the doctor's office. It's his way of bribing the doctor to give him a prescription. It works for nearly all of Dad's network of doctors in Chillicothe and the surrounding cities and towns of south-central Ohio.

However, even with a network of doctors, when you take this many Percodan, you are bound to need to go back to one sooner than normal.

Dad takes the fruit basket along with some excuse for losing the remainder of his pills, or they got stolen or whatever, and he gets another prescription.

We kids wait with Mom in the car while he's inside the doctor's office. He comes out of the office with script in hand, waving it at Mom and us, with a huge smile on his face.

There are also times he comes out with two bottles of pills in hand, the Percodan and the Valium, shaking them with joy. Some of the doctors' offices can fill the prescriptions. When they fill on site, Dad immediately opens the bottle of Percodan, dropping five of them into his hand, and takes them with his Pepsi, all right in front of us.

Sometimes, Dad comes out of the doctor's office looking all glum, pretending as though he didn't get anything. Then he pulls out the script or pill bottles with a laugh once in the car.

As a codependent or being stuck in the cycle, you take your queue from the addict, and you are always happy to see him break a smile coming out of the doctor's office or after his prank in the car. If he doesn't, which happens from time to time, it's some form of misery until he gets his fix. Meaning, he's just a real ass until he gets the next script filled.

I know today there are prescription drug monitoring programs. They try to help prevent this vicious cycle of doctor and pharmacy visits that leads to addiction. I only wish it had existed in our community back then or there had been some other way to see and stop the pattern.

Still to this day, I question whether the doctors knew he was addicted and kept on prescribing.

Maybe they felt pity on him?

Maybe they just took the fruit basket bribe?

Maybe they were bad doctors incentivized by the drug companies? The drama miniseries *PainKiller* comes to mind.

I guess I'll never know the answer to my questions, but it's tragic most of the doctors continued to write him scripts. I would have rather dealt with a real ass of a dad than see him waste his life by taking so many painkillers.

While in the white house, things only got worse, not better. Mom started taking painkillers too. She took Darvocet, which were less potent. She had back pain as well, not from surgery but likely from caring for five kids and helping Dad around the house. He was a big dude to try to carry around when passed out. Mom became addicted to Darvocet, although she didn't take as many as Dad.

Nonetheless, two addictions cost money. Valium sales weren't enough to cover prescription costs, gas or ride money to the doctor, fruit baskets, or whatever else.

No money meant hunger ensued the last week or so of each month. The welfare checks and food stamps were long gone, especially with a family of seven. Not much hope in the cycle. What was a kid to do?

5
The White House . . .
Of Distrust and Fraud

THANKFULLY, THERE WAS A GLIMMER of hope as I turned twelve.

I was super excited to take over a newspaper route in my neighborhood when another kid who had it moved away. I asked Mom to call the *Chillicothe Gazette* and see if I could have the route. They gave it to me!

Now I had a little extra money for candy, toys, or whatever a poor kid could dream of, right? All I had to do was take the stack of newspapers that were dropped off at my house, roll each one up, wrap it with a rubber band, stuff them all in my paper route bag they also provided, and then jump on my Pro Thunder bike and deliver away.

I was a great paperboy. I got to know my customers rather well.

For the younger families, I rode my bike and tossed the newspaper on their front porch, unless they requested to have it put in the newspaper holder of their mailbox. Most of the homes on my route had a front porch, and their mailboxes had a holder for newspapers.

For the elderly folks, I always hopped off my bike and put the newspaper in their newspaper holder or inside their front screen door somehow. I often thought of my grandparents when delivering to the elderly. I didn't want to overburden them with walking too far to get their newspaper, especially in the wintertime.

In the early 1980s, paperboys and papergirls went door-to-door at the beginning of each month to collect the money due for newspaper delivery. There was no such thing as online pay.

I had about seventy-five customers, so a lot of houses to get to, and it took some time. However, it was always worth it because this is how I got paid! You always collected more than the cost, and any tips you received were a bonus on top!

Much like mail carriers, you had to make your delivery, rain or shine, hot or cold, and if you wanted to get paid, you did your collections just the same.

One very snowy winter day, I'm out doing my collections. There's a good six inches or so of snow on the ground, and it's still snowing. Remember, I loved being outdoors, and riding my bike through the snow was awesome, so all in all, I am good. However, it's very cold. The Midwest wet kind of cold.

I'm about a mile from home when Dad pulls up in a car we just happen to have at the time. One or two of my sisters are with him along with Donnie. He calls me over to the car, which for a moment feels good as I feel the heat of the car spewing out the window.

Without saying hello or how are you doing or anything, he hands me a list of grocery items scribbled on a piece of scrap paper. He says Mom wants me to take my collection money and go buy the groceries on the list. He says she wants them this evening, right after I finish collecting, and it's starting to get dark. Yeah, you read it right.

Here I am, the youngest of the entire family, providing for the entire family. What the heck was that all about!

The list is long. Did I even have enough money for everything?

Mind you, not all the money I'm collecting is mine. I still need to pay the *Chillicothe Gazette*.

So I'm out here in the cold while they're in a warm car, and they want me to ride my bike for at least three miles to Jenny and Bankie's, all the way over on Water Street, to get groceries? Then I must carry the groceries while on my bike. That's a bunch of bull crap!

Yes, I was skilled at riding my bike with no hands, but it's freakin 'snowing out and almost dark!

What do you think I did? Yes, I rode to the store and got the groceries, but only because Mom wanted me to. I didn't want to disappoint her.

Later, I wondered if she was even the one asking. I'm betting she told Dad to take the list and get the groceries, but he passed it off to me. I can't remember who all was home when I got back from the store, but I know Dad wasn't there. All the better, I suppose, because I hated him for it.

There's more.

My newspaper customers tipped well even though money wasn't abundant in the east end of Chillicothe. Many of them were solid, blue-collar, hard-working families, and they appreciated a young man out doing his best to make some extra money. During Christmastime, they tipped very well, so I was able to save up quite a bit.

I had about a hundred dollars saved up as several customers gave me twenty-dollar bills as Christmas tips. It was a lot of money for a twelve-year-old, soon to be thirteen.

I'm thinking of all the things I can buy with the money. Some nice shoes and clothes, maybe a few toys. Unlike other kids, we didn't get new shoes and clothes at the start of the school year. It just wasn't in the budget, not that my parents even maintained a budget.

Trust was an issue in our house. Mom was the only person I trusted, and probably Donnie. I certainly didn't trust Dad, and my sisters were sketchy as well, at least to me.

So I hid my money underneath the carpet as you enter our bedroom. I checked on it every day to make sure it was still there, at least until I was ready to spend it. The hundred-plus dollars—in various twenties, tens, fives, and change—was organized by denominations. Yes, type A kid.

One day I was checking to make sure my money was still there, and it felt like someone was watching. I turned around and no one was there. My gut told me to change hiding places, but I was in a hurry and left it there. I should have listened to my gut.

The next day, when I checked on the money, it was almost all gone. There were a few dollars and some change left. Someone stole the paper route money from a twelve-year-old, after this same twelve-year-old bought groceries for them.

I immediately asked Mom about it. She said she didn't know who took it, but she had a look on her face. The look of uncertainty, which was like the uncertainty in her voice when I was five. She knew who took it.

It wasn't my sisters because no goods showed up from them in the next week or two, which would have been the case if they had taken it. However, Dad made a trip to the doctor soon after the money was taken. It was him!

I hated him for what he did to me as a five-year-old, but that's nothing compared to taking hard-earned money from a poor kid who had big plans with the money. I was traumatized and so confused by what happened.

Dad also did something to traumatize Mom, something as bad as him cheating on her, in my opinion.

Dad talked for years about getting a settlement check from workers' compensation for "back pay" due to him. They didn't start paying him right away from when he first filed a claim. Well, sure enough, a check finally came in. I don't remember the exact amount, but I think it was around $25,000. It was a ton of money for us, and it was an absolute free-for-all at our house for a while.

We ate Domino's pizza every night for like a month. When poor kids say they're getting tired of Dominos, you know they've been eating a lot of it. No grocery shopping for a while as we ate Sumburger's, tenderloin sandwiches, delivered by taxi, from Paint Grill, and of course some McDonald's thrown in there. I hadn't eaten that much in, well, forever.

Dad also used some of the money to buy a bunch of new furniture items, mainly for him and Mom. A new waterbed and bedroom furniture. New living room furniture. New TVs.

Of course, our neighbors were watching as these food and furniture delivery people showed up to our door for what seemed to us like every day for a couple of months.

You know what this means?

Envy, especially in a poorer neighborhood.

As it turns out, our neighbors, the very ones who took Dad to the doctor and got paid in pills, decided to turn us into the welfare department. Remember, we were on welfare and food stamps, so you guessed it, welfare fraud was the charge.

I guess it was Mom who signed up for welfare and food stamps because she was the one who got arrested. A felony charge, I suppose due to the amount of welfare dollars and food stamps we received for those few months while also receiving this other unclaimed workers' comp money. Even though Mom was not the direct recipient of the workers' comp money, her being married to Dad and the money coming into our household was the problem. Mom's name was in the paper and everything.

Now, granted, Mom benefited from the settlement check just as much as the rest of us, but she should not have had to take the fall for it. I later found out Dad told her not to report the extra household income to the Welfare Department. Dad got off free and clear. No arrest, nothing. Did he show any remorse? No. It just wasn't in his nature. Probably because he was just thinking of how much he contributed with his settlement check.

I hated him for allowing Mom to take the fall, despite how much "stuff" we got over those two to three months.

The good news was Mom had never been arrested before, so she received probation and only needed to pay back the few months of money we received plus some fines.

I prayed for her a few times during the whole ordeal. Maybe God was listening and would show mercy. Sure enough, they allowed her to make payments, which helped. However, it also meant we no longer qualified for welfare and food stamps. That sucked because the settlement check didn't last forever.

I don't know why, perhaps it was due to the embarrassment of the welfare fraud, but Dad and Mom decided we needed to move not long after Mom's sentencing. Dad still had a lot of money from the settlement check despite the spending spree, so he bought a brand new fourteen-by-seventy, four-bedroom mobile home, or trailer, as they were called in South Central Ohio.

Yeah, we were now going to likely be referred to as trailer trash, I suppose, but hey, for the first time ever, it was a new home! There weren't any trailer parks in town, so we needed to move to the far eastern end of Chillicothe. Thankfully, this happened as we were transitioning from middle school to high school in the summer of 1984, right around the time I was turning fourteen.

I say thankfully, but this is also a transition on top of another transition. Oh, and I had to give up my paper route as well, which was a bummer, but it wasn't as if I got to keep all the money anyway.

A few other things happened in the white house before we moved. I should mention them as I wrap up these two white house chapters since they either revealed my potential or had some impact on me.

Despite all the things happening, I had perfect attendance in both fifth and eighth grades. Heck, in fifth grade I was one of two captains of the school patrol, or crossing guard. You know, the kids (before adults) who wore a colored belt over their shoulder and around their waste, with a badge on it, no less, and guided kids across the street. The other captain was my friend, Jean. She was a good Captain too, and we had a lot of fun leading the school patrol teams of red and blue. I was very proud of these accomplishments.

Another development during this time was when Mom's sister, Aunt Maxine, and her husband, Uncle Hershel, and my cousins, Stevie and Tina, moved to Chillicothe. We started to hang out more, and Stevie and I became close. Aunt Maxine drove us around in a gigantic brown LTD we called the Brown Bomber. She took us down to Grandpa and Grandma Hill's house all the time. Stevie and I got into all sorts of shenanigans, which didn't help in my later teen years.

Somewhere in there, my oldest sister, Sally, got married to a guy named Bill and divorced shortly after. She moved out of the white house and then back in again. All the better, as Bill was a little bit crazy. He would shoot us with his BB gun. Before we moved, she found another boyfriend named Bob and moved out again. Bob was a good guy, but they eventually broke up.

My sister, Donna, also found a boyfriend, Johnnie, and moved in with him and his sister, Terry. They ended up moving into Grandpa Sparks's house once he moved in with my Aunt Maxine and Uncle Charlie. Grandpa began suffering from Alzheimer's. He always remembered me, though, for which I was grateful. I think it was because I'm the one who always went to him when I was younger. Donna and Johnnie are still together.

My sister, Angel, got pregnant and gave birth to my nephew, Jonathan. He was Dad and Mom's first grandchild. She didn't move out because she was only sixteen. She and Jonathan stayed with us, and Jonathan, who was nicknamed Bug Juice, quickly became the center of attention, especially for Dad. No resentment there at all with Dad's lack of attention toward me, as it was the beginning of him slowing down, still doing drugs but staying home more now. Plus, Jonathan was a good kid and cute as could be. He brought joy to all of us.

Of course, Donnie and I continued to hang out all the way up until we moved out of the white house. Street football, riding bikes, and swimming in rivers were all the rage. We threw baseball a lot too. I dreamed of being a big-league pitcher as most kids did. He caught for me as I pitched. He dubbed as an umpire at the same time, calling balls and strikes.

Unfortunately, I was a little hotheaded, and when he didn't call what I thought was a strike, I got mad at him, and we argued and quit. I was so stupid. I'm sorry, Donnie.

While at the white house, I also continued to pray.

"God, please don't let me have any bad dreams tonight."

However, one night not long before we moved, when Donnie and I still shared a bedroom, I was lying on my back, hands clasped between my belly and chest, praying.

"What are you doing?" Donnie asked curiously. Maybe he'd noticed me doing this before, as I did it every night, but this was the first time he asked me about it.

I quickly said, "Nothing." I finished up, and it was the last time I prayed for a long time.

I had a prayer streak of nearly eight years, every night the same thing with the occasional extra prayers thrown in there, and just like that, it ended. Maybe it's because I was getting older and felt I didn't need to pray any longer? I wasn't afraid of bad dreams anymore. Those were kid prayers.

Maybe I was embarrassed to say what I was doing?

Maybe I just denied God for the first time? If so, it wouldn't be the last time.

Why didn't I tell Donnie what I was doing? Was I afraid he'd laugh at me if I told him what I was praying about?

What if he told my friends and they all made fun of me?

Or was it the nearly four years of distrust and fraud in the white house that made me give up hope in praying?

I like to think God was with me when I prayed, protecting me, which it seemed he did, as I didn't have a single bad dream during that time.

Regardless, I had stopped praying. So now what?

6
The Trailer: Darker

YES, THIS NEW "HOUSE" HAD a color too, beige, but we just referred to it as the trailer. I had slept over at Grandpa and Grandma Hill's trailer before, but I had never lived in a trailer. This one being brand-new seemed like an upgrade to me. No roaches, rats, and far less space to cool or heat. Unless, of course, you can't afford propane, which sometimes we couldn't.

Even though the trailer was new, our family dynamics were the same, and our social status hadn't changed. We were still poor with drug-addicted parents, and the settlement money Dad received was running out fast, especially after the purchase of the trailer.

This meant we didn't have nice clothes and certainly no new clothes to wear to high school. It made it difficult to "fit in" at high school with a bunch of "rich kids" from the west end.

The high school was a mix of kids from Mt. Logan Middle School, poorer east-end kids, and Smith Middle School, wealthier west-end kids. Some of our east-end friends figured out ways to adapt and fit in. Then there were others who no longer wanted to hang out with their east-end brethren, which made things even more difficult.

Coming into puberty, moving into a new neighborhood, and starting high school at the same time proved too much for me.

During my freshman year of the 1984–'85 school season, I went from practically all straight A's up through eighth grade, and perfect attendance in eighth grade, to C's and below with attendance far from perfect. I also started to get a bad case of acne. It made me reclusive, and I got in touch with my introverted side quick.

Around the same time, I figured out how to get twelve free cassettes for a penny through Columbia House. I never did purchase the required number to order after the dozen for a penny. My own and first instance of fraud, I guess. I'm sorry, Columbia House.

I can't remember the other eleven cassettes, but there was one cassette I played repeatedly. It was Billy Idol's *Rebel Yell*, with songs such as "Eyes Without a Face," "Flesh for Fantasy," "White Wedding," "Dancing with Myself," and many more great songs.

I also started taking Dad's *Playboy* magazines and putting up the centerfolds all over my bedroom. The demon from my early childhood of seeing those magazines all over the place had come full circle and was now thriving in the trailer.

I'm not sure why Mom allowed it. Maybe she felt hypocritical asking me to take them down considering they belonged to Dad. Or maybe she just didn't know what to do other than watch me go through all these emotional phases as a young teenager.

With all these things combined, a path started to form for me, a darker path.

For the stories I'm about to share in the remainder of this chapter and the next two chapters, I'm not going to use real names unless they're family or friends I know don't mind. I hope to preserve the dignity of the others by doing so.

Beginning to alienate from Donnie, I felt desperate for friendship. I met some kids who were a grade ahead of me, sophomores, Blake and Jack. Both lived in the trailer park. Blake's grandparents managed the trailer park. They and Blake's mom also owned a bar, which sat at the entrance to the trailer park.

Blake had access to a little more money than we did. Jack was as poor as we were. Both were accepting of me and Donnie, so we began to hang out a bit, me more than Donnie.

Then it began. It was a Friday evening. Blake and Jack asked if I wanted to have some beers. Right next to our trailer was a red-and-white barn used for storage. It was the perfect place to sneak around and have a few beers. I think Blake put up the cash to buy the beer, and his older half brother, Tony, made the purchase for us. A six-pack.

My very first beer was an Old Milwaukee Best Light. A six-pack meant two beers each. Having never had beer except for the occasional drink a Generation X kid takes from an uncle, Grandpa, or some stranger, drinking two full cans in about fifteen minutes was enough for me to get buzzed.

We walked out of the barn and started doing cartwheels in the lawn just behind our trailer. Although the process of acquiring a taste for beer, and especially for Old Milwaukee Best Light was a grueling one, the buzz certainly felt good and made it worth it.

When it was time to go inside, we found some gum and chomped on it for a little while to help take the beer smell away. I'm not sure where Dad was, but Mom was watching the news, always her routine before going to bed. I came inside and went straight to my room so I wouldn't say anything to her and she couldn't smell the beer. She didn't say anything, and I'm pretty sure she didn't notice.

There were several more rounds of beers in the weeks to follow. I'm not exactly sure how long the progression took, maybe a month or so, but marijuana was next up on the list of things to try.

I referenced earlier Dad bought marijuana smoking kits for Sally and Donna, which implied they smoked marijuana. They did. They also shared a toke or two with Donnie and me at the white house. Again, it's one of those Generation X things that just sort of happened. However, taking a toke and smoking a whole joint are quite different. The habit eventually turned into smoking entire joints, but it started smaller.

Blake and I were hanging out at his sister's trailer. She was away somewhere, but she left some roaches in the ash tray. No, not cockroaches, but rather tiny remains of marijuana cigarettes referred to as roaches.

Blake asked if I wanted to try some. Already a few beers in, I said yes. We smoked a half dozen or so roaches, which meant a good ten to fifteen tokes each.

I was high.

I remember taking a single toke or two as a ten- or eleven-year-old and just running around acting crazy, but these tokes, and this many, brought on a serious buzz like I hadn't experienced before.

Phil Collins's "Sussudio" was playing on the radio. Blake started dancing away. It's a great song, so I started dancing too. I'm sure we looked like fools, especially me, this pimple-faced, introverted teenager, but we didn't care. A dual buzz was going, and we were having a great time. The smells of beer and marijuana escaped my parents again at the end of the night, or perhaps they did notice and decided to let it slide.

It gets darker.

Remember the Valium Dad got with his Percodan? Why not give those a try?

I knew where Dad kept his pill bottles. They were in his bedroom closet, up on a top shelf. I'm not sure how I knew, but it seemed like a good hiding place.

One evening, I found them. I counted ten out of a very full bottle. I was sure he'd blame Sally or Donna if he even counted how many were in there.

Ten Valium seemed like a good number to take so I could share some with my friends. What I can't remember is how many I took or how many I shared. I just know by the next day, all ten were gone, and I really don't remember anything other than what Sally and Donna told me.

Apparently, I was in the back seat of someone's car, all Valium sloppy from taking too many. You know, half-asleep, slurred speech, dreary eyes, all slumped over. I didn't seem to acknowledge or even know Sally or Donna. They were pretty upset with me.

I'm not sure where Donnie was when all of this happened. Probably avoiding me like the plague. He was the smart one who stayed away from the hard stuff.

Anyway, I think I gave one or two Valium away and took the rest. Way too many for a fourteen-year-old.

How many Valiums do you have to take to overdose?

What if it was mixed with alcohol or marijuana, which was likely a part of the evening cocktail considering we had been both drinking and smoking up to this point?

What if I went back in the trailer for more from Dad's pill bottle?

What if I tripped or stumbled over something and hit my head and bled to death?

What if I just stopped breathing altogether?

I'm sure there would have been an obscure article in the *Chillicothe Gazette* the next day about a young, troubled teenager who overdosed or died by a tragic accident because of drugs.

As I reflect on this moment in my life, I wonder who was looking out for me. I could have died of any number of things that night.

Was I being spared for something else? Or did I just get lucky?

Yes, as a kid I jumped off train trestles into rivers, jumped off high roofs into yards, climbed to the top of trees only to have the branch break and fall all the way down, but this was different. I was coherent and just being adventurous during all those other things. On Valium, I was completely incoherent and all stoned out.

It's difficult to process because I do think this was my first real escape from death. Somehow, I was saved, spared.

Did I learn a lesson?

Unfortunately, no.

Well, I think I backed off the pills for a little bit, but it later became a bragging right.

There was more exploring to do.

7
The Trailer: Darkest

REMEMBER BLAKE'S OLDER BROTHER, TONY? He was cool to hang out with, so Jack and I and sometimes Blake went over to his trailer and hung out with Tony and his wife, Tanya.

Tanya was in her early twenties, super sweet and very pretty. I had a huge crush on her as a teenager. Tony was cool, but it was just as much fun being around Tanya. She had a beautiful smile and a great laugh.

Friday nights at Tony and Tanya's meant *Miami Vice*. Who didn't watch *Miami Vice* during this time? The intro by Phil Collins was, wow, good stuff.

Tony was into all the things we were into as far as drinking and drugs, and he didn't hesitate to contribute to the delinquency of minors with plenty of alcohol and marijuana. He also took us to the next level and introduced us to smoking cocaine.

No, it wasn't crack; it was freebasing.

Oh, the irony. Freebasing cocaine while watching *Miami Vice*, hoping Sonny and Rico didn't come busting through the door to arrest us.

What else was there in the drugs category after freebasing?

Tony talked about shooting up all the time but said it was for addicts. He joked about shooting up between your toes so no one noticed track marks on your arm.

Do you know how people who always talk about or degrade something are likely the ones who are doing it?

Tanya always told him he better never do it. I think she was fearful he might, and in hindsight, she was likely fearful of what he'd become if he kept going further and what harm it would bring not just to him but to her as well.

One day, Tony stopped by our trailer to see if I was home. I came to the door, and he said he wanted to show me something.

I went with him.

We went upstairs in the barn. He said he started shooting up and wanted to show me how it was done. I'd seen it on TV before but never in real life.

I started to get nervous.

He wrapped a band around his arm, above the elbow. He poured something into a spoon and "cooked" it with his lighter.

He pulled out a syringe and drew the liquid into it. He looked me directly in the eye and asked if I want to try it too.

"No, man, I'm good."

He didn't argue or try to persuade me further, but he asked if I could pull the band tighter as it loosened. I reluctantly agreed, as at this moment I really wanted to be out of the barn and away from this situation.

He then injected the substance, and after a few seconds, he murmured for me to release the band.

I released it.

I stayed with Tony for maybe five minutes or less, as he had this glazed look on his face. I wanted to make sure he was okay. I considered him a friend. I then told him I had to go, saying I heard Mom calling.

I lied.

Still murmuring, "All right, cool. Hey, don't say anything to Tanya."

"Sure, man."

I took off out of there.

A couple days later, I saw Tanya outside. She looked troubled. She called for me and said she wanted to ask me a question.

I knew what it was about.

She asked if I thought Tony was shooting up.

"I don't know, Tanya."

I lied.

I don't know why I lied. Maybe selfishly I didn't want to break up our fun *Miami Vice* Friday evenings.

I was also afraid of Tony, probably just as much as Tanya was afraid. I thought he would beat us up if we crossed him. He could get amped at times, and I could see he had a mean streak to him. On occasion we saw Tanya with bruises and suspected Tony may have beaten her.

Much later in life, he did.

Tony was charged and convicted of beating Tanya to death.

Tragic, and such a senseless loss of life and the loss of a beautiful soul.

Perhaps if I hadn't lied to her, she could have gotten out earlier, and it could have possibly saved her life. I don't know, maybe.

Either way, I'm sorry, Tanya.

I wish I hadn't lied to you. You deserved to know the truth. You were such a good friend to us, and I shouldn't have lied to you.

I'm sorry.

As I reflect on this moment in the barn with Tony, I wonder if it was the second time someone was looking out for me.

What kept me from taking the next step and shooting up?

I mean, heck, I was already progressing my drug use at a strong pace through my freshman and sophomore years living at the trailer park. Shooting up seemed like a logical next step. It could have also been a fatal one.

Who knew what was in the spoon and how my body may have reacted to it?

Who knew if Tony's blood was already tainted, and if it might have tainted mine, too, if we shared a needle? He only had one needle.

I will never know, and I'm okay with it. I'm just thankful something or someone helped me to respond with, "No man, I'm good."

Although I didn't take the next step of intravenous drugs, I was still very much into all the other things.

I had a hard time looking at Tony the same way after what happened in the barn, so we didn't hang out as much. I started to hang out more with Jack and some other fellas. Willie, Rick, Rob, Todd, and a few others, all jean-jacket, east-end partiers.

Jack and I skipped school occasionally and hung out with Rick, who was a few years older than we were and no longer in school. He was cool. He also somehow managed to get on welfare and food stamps, so we would get stoned and then buy a bunch of chips and other junk food with the food stamps to take care of our munchies. Rick's house was pretty much the party house, and we crashed there quite a bit.

My final grades as a freshman weren't good. I'm sure the C's or whatever acceptable grades I got were a social promotion more than anything because I really didn't focus in class or do a lot of homework.

I was also getting zeros and certainly not doing any homework during a three-day suspension for fighting.

Some kid named Robbie broke my pencil, so I punched him in the face and rammed his head into the wall. I nearly blinded him because he was wearing glasses when I hit him. The broken glasses not only left a gash on one of my right knuckles but also right next to Robbie's left eye. Over a pencil. Stupid.

I'm sorry, Robbie.

After my freshman year, we partied all summer of 1985 right into the start of my sophomore year in the fall.

I walked into Spanish 2 on day one, sat down briefly, and walked right out with a girl named Tracy when the teacher started speaking Spanish. We didn't remember anything from Spanish 1, so we went to the guidance counselor's office to get assigned a different class.

I took the easiest classes I possibly could my sophomore year just to get through it. It was much of the same through my entire sophomore year, barely making it through school and partying all the time.

There was a volunteer Scared Straight program the school held at the Chillicothe Correctional Institute (CCI). I volunteered to go just to get out of school, and I wanted to see what the inside of the prison looked like.

An inmate named Big Cig said all kinds of expletives to me and what he'd do to me if I ever ended up in there. Sure, I was a little "scared" of what it might be like should Big Cig get a hold of me, but all in all, it didn't have the desired effect of deterring me from anything I was into.

I started taking seeds from the weed I got and planting them to grow marijuana. They typically made it to about a foot or so tall, and I replanted them out in the woods by the trailer park. They ended up getting eaten by animals or stolen.

I was much better at pinching enough weed for several joints from quarter-, half-, or full-ounce bags I purchased as a middleman. Yes, I was a small-time drug dealer as well.

My friend Todd's dad sold weed but only allowed a small handful of Todd's friends to buy from him. People who wanted it drove me there, and I went inside to get it. I'd hit the bathroom before heading back out to the car, pinching whatever I wanted. Then I gave them the supposed full purchase when I got back to the car.

As any good purchaser did, they also gave me a pinch for a joint or two as a way of saying thank you. Sometimes they looked at the bag thinking it looked a little light. Perhaps I got too greedy and pinched too much, but they still pinched me off something.

Yeah, it was wrong, but at this stage of my life I didn't care. I just wanted to have enough to smoke and to sell for extra money.

So, in addition to doing the drugs, I was now dealing the drugs. I also stole some of Dad's Percodan and Valium from time to time and sold them.

I pretty much hit what I thought was rock bottom until Tony asked Jack and me to break into the bar with him. His own grandparents' and mom's bar, mind you.

Jack and I thought it would be cool because we could have access to all the liquor in there and maybe get some money as well. There was no money, but there was lots of liquor and some other things Tony kept stashed at his trailer, and we drank with him for several months to come.

Tony never got caught, and we didn't either. I guess no one ever suspected a son would rob his own grandparents and mother.

Blake was really upset and asked all of us if we knew anything. He asked Jack and me, Willie, and even Donnie. By this point, Jack and I had pretty good poker faces and just played stupid, saying we didn't know anything, that we were just hanging out in my room all evening.

I lied.

In this case, I know why I lied.

I'm sorry, Blake, and if it can ever make a difference, I'm willing to pay for whatever the loss was that night.

I'm sure we stole enough to make it a felony. Yes, the statute of limitations has long passed, especially for minors committing a crime, but nonetheless, I now had burglary to add to my downward-spiral résumé.

In hindsight, I'm so grateful we didn't get caught.

What if we did?

I would have had something on my record, an official juvenile delinquent who may have ended up in juvenile hall. It could have meant an eventual path to CCI.

Was someone looking out for me again, or did I just get lucky?

Dad and Mom suspected I might have been involved. I found out later, this situation along with my continued rebellious behavior got them thinking we should move. Well, that and the fact Dad had fallen behind on lot rent.

So, after my sophomore year at Chillicothe High School and after Dad's pleading with Tony and his grandpa to move the trailer, they hooked it up to their trailer-towing big rig, drove it up to a lot Dad had somehow secured in the small town of Yellowbud, and dumped it there. When I say dumped it, they basically backed it into the slot, unhooked it, and left.

It was up to Dad to figure out how to hook everything up, water, electricity, etc. and to figure out how to balance the thing and then anchor it down. He did eventually, and after essentially being evicted again, we started the next chapter of our lives there in Yellowbud, which was pretty much in the middle of nowhere.

I'm sure my parents thought long and hard about getting out of the city of Chillicothe where I was into so much mischief.

Would making me a country mouse do the trick?

Would moving me away from all those bad influences do the trick?

Would a new school, Unioto High School, do the trick?

Or would the demons and darkness still reside in the trailer as it sat in a new lot?

8
Yellowbud:
Bottom of the Barrel

NO, IT WASN'T SOME NEW weed I could smoke, although it's what I thought when I first heard the name of where we were moving to. Yellowbud is a very small rural community between the towns of Chillicothe and Circleville, Ohio. Dad and Mom thought it would be a good idea to move us there, mainly to get me out of the "city" of Chillicothe and hopefully out of trouble.

We only lived there a year, but there were some significant moments during this time. Perhaps you thought I hit the bottom of the barrel at the trailer. Well, not quite.

Living in Yellowbud meant we were no longer in the Chillicothe school district. Instead, we transferred to Unioto High School. It was about ten miles from Yellowbud to Unioto High School, so we took the bus every day. It was a long bus ride as it made its way down different farm roads to pick up kids who lived around the area of Yellowbud.

Donnie started making friends right away; most of whom lived in Yellowbud. There was Chuck, Craig, Todd, Erin, Shelby, Susie, and several others. Although I saw these kids from time to time, this was really Donnie's crew, and many of them still are to this day. I eventually got to know them better, but I also made some new friends who lived either closer to the school or farther away from Yellowbud.

It's interesting how you can take a "stoner" out of the city, but you can't take the stoner out of the kid. I identified a new group of stoner friends at Unioto. There was Brent, Doug, Jared, James, and Jon. There were others, too, but this was the main crew.

For whatever reason, I was also noticed by more girls at Unioto. Maybe it was the "new kid" effect because I wasn't any cuter than before, and my personality hadn't changed from school to school. I sort of dated a couple of girls, but not really. I was way too focused on getting high.

My new crew had just as much access to beer, weed, pills, and everything else you can imagine. The one thing that changed was not waiting until weeknights and weekends to party. I started getting high at school, smoking marijuana at lunch.

We had a whole system set up where we smoked behind the school along a back wall with no doors or windows. There were usually three or four of us together, so we traded off as lookouts on either end of this part of the building, as the back entrances to the school were around each corner and a short walk away. We could easily see the principal, Mr. Warren, or any other teacher coming with plenty of time to get rid of whatever we were smoking. We got high first thing at lunch period and then grabbed some lunch to take care of the munchies.

James and I had history class right after lunch, and we'd be high going in there. I can't remember the teacher's name, but he didn't seem to care much. We think he got high as well—not during school hours, but during weeknights and weekends. Maybe he was empathetic toward us fellow stoners. Regardless, history was boring, so it was a tough class to be high in, especially as the buzz wore off.

So basically, Dad and Mom's plan to get me away from the drugs didn't work. I still drank and smoked more marijuana than anything, but then I was introduced to lysergic acid diethylamide, or LSD, which is the drug's street name. This opened a whole different world because I wasn't just high; I was what they call tripping. The LSD suddenly became my go-to drug, and I was tripping with my crew what seemed like every weekend.

I can't reference any scientific studies, but I can only imagine how much the LSD and all the other drugs adversely affected my brain development and functionality at the time. I do know with LSD there can be longer-term issues, such as hallucinogen persisting perception disorder (HPPD) or severe schizophrenia. Thankfully, I don't suffer from any of these conditions. Given how much of it I did, I often wonder why this is.

As if that wasn't enough, my friends were turning of age to drive, so there were many times we were in a car or on a motorcycle either drunk, stoned, or tripping.

I was tripping and riding on the back of a motorcycle with Doug doing at least a hundred miles per hour down Route 104. Any little slip of his hand or an animal crossing the road or you name it could have sent us flying to our deaths. This was just one instance of probably dozens more.

My friends and I could have been a potential headline so many times over. Somehow I was spared, and thankfully I didn't kill anyone as I committed these crimes. I often tell people, who today look at me with surprise when they learn of my rebellious youth, there are so many times I should have died. Yet I didn't.

Perhaps a blessing in disguise is a suspension I received during the latter part of my junior year.

It was a very, very rainy spring day, pouring rain outside. Jon and I were somehow excused to go to the bathroom at the same time. Not good and surely trouble was coming.

"Man, it's f#@&!ng raining hard, Jon!"

"Yeah, and you know what would be funny? If you pull the fire alarm and everyone has to go outside in the rain."

"Dude, we'll get in big trouble."

"Not if you don't get caught. Come on, dude. I dare you."

Well, that's all it took, a dare from Jon.

We quickly decided on which alarm to pull and our escape route, which was to run into the bathroom, where we should have been in the first place.

I pulled the alarm, and we bolted. However, Mr. Bradley just happened to be standing by his classroom door not far from the bathroom. He saw us running into the bathroom.

Busted!

He ran in, knowing we did it, and he dragged us down to Mr. Warren's office and placed us in two separate rooms. I think Mr. Bradley broke school fire alarm protocol by letting us stay inside. Or maybe Mr. Bradley didn't want to go outside. Either way, the entire school went outside until the fire department gave the all-clear.

It's probably thirty minutes later but it seemed like an eternity when Mr. Warren finally came into his office. He's a bald man and had rainwater running off his head. His suit was absolutely soaked. He threw his keys across the room and screamed something at me to the effect of "What the hell do you think you're doing?"

I can't even remember what else he said. All I know is I've never seen a principal or teacher so pissed in my life. I really thought he was going to punch me or, worse, kill me.

I uttered an "I don't know."

It's true. I really didn't know what the hell I was doing. I was just a stupid kid, a stoner, not thinking at all.

Jon got a three-day suspension for being an accomplice. I got a ten-day suspension for the actual act. I was later told Mr. Warren initially wanted me charged with a crime. It was either a first-degree misdemeanor or a fifth-degree felony depending on if there was economic harm over $1,000. I'm sure he could have easily come up with this amount in lost teacher salary, school hours, fire department costs, or whatever.

I was also told he wanted to expel me from Unioto High School. I'm sure he had every right to do so, at a minimum.

So why just a ten-day suspension? I was spared a potential criminal record. I was spared an expulsion, which would have set me even further back than I already was in school. Once again, I was spared.

Dad and Mom were mad at me, but they didn't really punish me. I couldn't see my friends and couldn't go anywhere with them. They said I was confined to Yellowbud, and I had to stay at the trailer during the day.

I just hung out and listened to music, so it wasn't too bad. Believe it or not, I did reflect on what I had done. I didn't change a whole lot, but I did back it off, just a bit.

During the weekend in the middle of my suspension, I still wasn't allowed to leave Yellowbud. I was bored and asked Mom where Donnie was. She said he was over at Chuck's house. I didn't even know where Chuck lived other than a general location, but I didn't have anything else to do, so I went looking for them.

I may or may not have smoked half a joint along the way, which delayed me a bit, but I eventually found them hanging out in Chuck's garage drinking beers. The only way I found them was overhearing their loud voices and bantering back and forth about some nonsense.

I knocked on the door, and to their surprise, there I was in their midst. I said something to the effect of "What's up? Can I hang out with you guys for a little while?"

To my surprise they were very welcoming, smiling a bit, too, remembering I sent all their asses out into the rain just days ago. Craig was especially welcoming since he liked to smoke weed, and he knew I usually had some. All was good, and I was happy to be hanging out.

What was most rewarding about this moment, and why I'll never forget it, is after nearly three long years I discovered my brother again. There he was, his usual funny self, drinking a beer and having a good time. It was at this moment I realized how much I missed him.

I had seriously gone off the rails and strayed far, far away from what we shared before high school, only thinking of myself and being selfish all this time. I almost didn't come back from the journey. Yet he welcomed me into his friend group.

Yes, I started to hang out more and become friends with his crew of Chuck, Todd, Craig, and Erin, who are all there in the garage, but most importantly, I started hanging out with Donnie again.

I'm sorry I went away for a few years there, Donnie. Thank you for welcoming back the prodigal son.

The track record for my junior year at Unioto High School ended up including a new drug, multiple should-have-died moments out with friends, C's, D's and F's, and a grand total of thirty-three missed days of school. Somehow, someone, somewhere declared I should still be a senior the next school year. Don't ask me how they came to this conclusion. Social promotion perhaps? Get him the hell out of here, or once again, I was spared.

During the year, I don't think much changed with Dad either, although he started to slow down. Either way, it was decided we were moving back to Chillicothe.

I think it was a twofold reason with us being out of money because Dad sold the trailer for cash, and their plan to save me from the city hadn't worked. I got way worse. I also think Mom didn't like living so far away from Chillicothe and most of her family there.

So, in the summer of 1987, we moved back to Chillicothe, to Johnson Road in the west end, to be exact. Yeah, east-enders in the west end. Donnie and I would finish our senior year together at Chillicothe High School, with a few twists and turns along the way, of course.

As I reflect on all my shenanigans in all "The Trailer" and "Yellowbud" chapters, I recall a few times getting into some serious, scary situations and calling out to God silently. You may know how the prayer goes.

"God, please get me out of this mess. I promise I won't do it again if you help me."

Even though I almost always did it again, I think God heard me. I was spared, many times over. I was sincere, at least in the moment. I just kept screwing up after the moment. Eventually I learned, right?

There were turning points ahead, perhaps where things started to sink in.

I hope.

9
Turning Points:
One

IT WAS NICE BEING BACK in Chillicothe, and Johnson Road meant we were living in the fancy west end, or at least fancy to us. We were still very much east-enders. Nonetheless, the house was cool, and I had an entire upstairs, rather secluded, part-loft, part-attic bedroom. It was perfect for me to continue to smoke weed, drink, trip, or do whatever.

Being it was summer and school was out meant constant partying. Essentially, a continuation of Yellowbud but back in Chillicothe. Donnie's crew from Yellowbud came into town quite a bit to drink. I also reconnected with some of my fellow east-end friends. We were doing a lot of LSD, with my own use being funded by profits from what I was selling at the time.

We also started attending a few parties at homes of west-end kids. Remember, these were the kids we hadn't quite fit in with when we became freshmen at Chillicothe High School.

I was at one party with a buddy named Shane. The girl's parents were hosting an adult party at the main house and allowing their daughter and her friends to drink and party along the driveway area. To use the bathroom, you had to go to the main house, and while doing so, I saw the adults smoking weed, including this girl's parents.

So once back with the teenagers, I decided to light up a joint. I was immediately chastised by the daughter, who said something of the effect, "We don't do that crap here. Put it away." I thought to myself, *You hypocritical bitch. Your parents are smoking it right now in the house.* I was ready to walk, but Shane was trying to stay in tight with these west-end kids, so I endured their hypocrisy.

As it turned out, west end wasn't any better than east end. They just lived in nicer houses.

When I was at home, and not long after we moved in at Johnson Road, I began noticing a cute girl who lived directly behind our house. The girl next door was named Becky, and she sunbathed out in her backyard quite a bit since it was summer. I was about to turn seventeen, and of course everything was raging at this point, especially for this undisciplined teenager. As such, an infatuation grew, and we began to talk.

Now, Becky and Donnie will deny it, but she liked him first, and I believe she talked to him long before she ended up talking to me. Perhaps it was his charm and sense of humor, or perhaps he was just home more often than I was and more accessible. We may never know, but as it turns out, he was probably way more disciplined than I and smart to avoid any senior-year relationships, especially with an underclassman. She was just a freshman, but a fifteen-year-old freshman.

Things progressed rather quickly once we mutually took an interest in each other. It wasn't necessarily a summer of love, as that just wasn't my mindset at the time, but we did spend a lot of time together. I snuck in and out of her house, which was not easy, and she snuck in and out of my house, which was very easy and not really sneaking.

As much as I didn't want to admit it, Becky became my steady girlfriend as I was about to start my senior year. She seemed chill, didn't do drugs, and didn't judge my own alcohol and drug abuse, although I'm not sure she was fully aware of just how much I did.

Like I said, I was still partying quite a bit that summer. Looking back at that time of my life, I wonder if God, though surely not approving of my premarital sexual relationship with Becky, somehow used the situation to slow me down. If I'm being honest, relationships can have a way of doing that, right?

Whatever it was, the next thing I remember, it was late summer, and I had been out partying hard the night before. I don't remember who I had been with. It's sad, I know, but I woke up the next morning in bed lying flat on my back, alive after another wild night.

I stared up at my Ronnie James Dio poster on the sloped ceiling. I was so into Dio and Ozzy Osbourne at that time. I softly spoke to myself in a rather raspy voice, having smoked weed all night.

"Man, what the hell am I doing? I really need to get my shit together."

This was turning point number one.

Here I was, now seventeen, about to start my senior year, and I had this moment in the middle of absolute chaos after three straight years of intense partying, alcohol and drug use, and multiple near death or "I should have died" experiences.

How does that happen?

Perhaps a better question is who made that happen?

In my opinion, there is no way in hell the prompt came from me, even though I voiced it. However, there is a way in heaven. God was calling.

To be clear, in that moment, I did not think it was a God thing. I didn't say a prayer. I didn't feel anything different. I just had the thought that I was about to start my senior year and I needed to figure out what to do before it was too late.

I didn't want to end up like Dad.

When I share this story, I often tell people that in hindsight I think God figuratively picked me up and turned me in the right direction.

It was kind of like how Zeus stood up Perseus after he collapsed from exhaustion in the original *Clash of the Titans* movie in 1981. That way Perseus could then go save Andromeda from the sea Titan by turning it into stone with Medusa's head.

Well, maybe not, but just as dramatic in the spiritual realm, I'm sure.

So now what?

Well, like I said, it wasn't a spiritual moment for me where I went cold turkey on everything bad in my life and started going to church. However, I did start to take note of what I needed to do to get my life in order and evaluate how I could further better my life. I also stopped making rash decisions. I still partied, but I started to back off the hard stuff like the pills and LSD.

This first turning point was off to a good start.

10
Turning Points:
Two

SCHOOL WAS NOW STARTING, SO I got enrolled in what I considered the most basic courses for a senior. No AP classes for me. I had to ease back into this whole studying thing, as I'd pretty much been on a three-year hiatus from any scholarly activity. It was cool, though, as I had already made up my mind that I wasn't going to go to college. No money for that, and I didn't have the grades for it anyway.

As a senior, you're pretty much on top of the world. I had quite a few friends, and I knew a lot of girls. So, when Becky saw me talking with them in the hallways or at a lunch table, she got quite jealous and possessive, which was not cool. It got to the point where to me she seemed a bit psychotic about the whole thing. I decided to break it off, or at least I tried.

Becky still tried to talk with me and occasionally said some nasty things, but for the most part I just ignored her and went about my business.

It wasn't that easy, especially being a seventeen-year-old boy and regularly thinking about sex. So the sneaking in and out of each other's houses continued over the next several months. In some of those instances, what may have started as protected sex ended up as unprotected sex.

Aside from the official breakup with Becky, I was doing well in school, back to A's and B's. Again, the courses weren't too difficult, but that was a major accomplishment after being in the C–F lane for the last three years.

I also continued to reflect on my first turning point moment in late summer. I knew I needed discipline and a whole lot more structure in my life.

About that same time, my cousin Stevie, who was like me in more ways than one, also needing discipline and structure, decided to join the United States Marine Corps. He asked me to consider enlisting with the idea that perhaps someday we could be stationed in the same location. We were close, and the military seemed like a strong option given my situation. So I decided to visit a couple of recruiters to explore options.

Stevie's recruiter, Staff Sergeant Walker, was the first recruiter I met. He was a Reconnaissance Marine who absolutely hated recruiting. He did a quick ASVAB pretest, which I guess I did okay on, as he said I qualified for a few desk jobs if that was the sort of thing I was looking for.

Stevie had signed up for infantry. I told Staff Sergeant Walker I wasn't interested in infantry. He then proceeded to tell me it didn't matter what job I took as all Marines are riflemen and I could die at any moment.

I think that was his way of trying to quickly weed out those who might not be able to hack it. He was very much a no-nonsense Marine. He wasn't about to BS me or offer a bunch of incentives to get me to join.

I told him I wanted to give it some thought.

That same day I decided to visit the United States Navy recruiter also. It was a way different experience. I don't remember the dude's name, which is probably a good thing, but he was seriously lax. He didn't seem all that interested in my questions and wasn't convincing at all. He did throw around a few incentives, but I kept thinking to myself, *This dude is not nearly as sharp, impressive, or straightforward as Staff Sergeant Walker.*

I ruled out the Navy quick.

I had heard the U.S. Coast Guard was pretty much like the Navy, and I heard the U.S. Air Force was for smart people. So I didn't even bother to visit those recruiters. That said, I still needed to think about it.

I took a couple of days.

To me, college wasn't an option, although I did think about it since several friends were going that route. I also didn't want to take the SAT or ACT because I knew I hadn't studied hard enough through high school to do well. I also didn't want to continue my current track either, suspecting that if I did, I would end up either a burnout or dead at some point soon.

A job at the Mead paper mill or Kenworth trucking didn't have any appeal either, although several friends went that route and were quite successful.

To break this cycle and funk of the last three years, I needed to do something extraordinary. I kept coming back to the need for discipline and structure, and of course, the military was appealing since Stevie was also joining.

I decided on the United States Marine Corps.

That was turning point number two, all in the span of a few months. It was one of the very best turning points and decisions of my life.

A couple of days later, I went back out to the recruiting station to share my decision with Staff Sergeant Walker. I told him again I didn't want infantry and asked if I could get guaranteed an "admin" type job. He said based on my pretesting he thought I could, but quickly reminded me I would be a Marine first and could die at any moment.

I think he just liked saying that, although I'm sure he wanted to be sure I was sure. Then we started the initial paperwork.

After getting through name, date of birth, SSN, address, etc., he had a few questions.

"Have you ever been arrested?"

"No, sir."

If you think about it, isn't that a miracle in and of itself after all the shenanigans I pulled over the past three years?

"Have you ever done any sort of illegal substances?"

I knew this question was coming because Stevie told me he, too, got the same question and gave an appropriate answer. However, it still caught me off guard for a moment, so I asked a clarifying question to buy time.

"Does being around other people who are smoking marijuana in confined spaces like a car or small room count?"

"No, it doesn't as long as you didn't smoke it."

"Then no, I haven't done illegal substances."

"Are you sure," he asked, "because they will require a drug test?"

"Yes," I said with as straight a face as possible. I had on my notorious stoner Levi jean jacket, so I'm sure he thought I was lying.

Of course I was lying.

Now, before you judge Staff Sergeant Walker or me, know that he asked a question, and I provided an answer. He did his job and annotated the answer I gave him, even if he had reservations. That is not an integrity violation since the next step before contract signing is a urinalysis test to prove whether a potential poolee, or newly enlisted recruit, is currently using illegal substances.

As for me, yes, I did lie. Yes, that was an integrity violation with an organization that prides itself on having the utmost integrity. However, the fact is, and this is not an excuse, at that time it was what I thought to be the only way to get into the Marines free and clear with a fresh start and no record of my deplorable past three years.

I learned later I could have possibly entered on a drug waiver, but possibly not for the types of drugs I had used. I may have had no chance of getting in, and I may have been stuck, or at least that's how I viewed it at the time. Stuck in the cycle.

I wanted out. I wanted something different and better. There was nothing going to stop me at this point.

Staff Sergeant Walker said he'd send through the initial paperwork to get things going, which could take a few weeks. This meant I had to cut out all the illegal substances so I could piss clean when I went to the Military Entrance Processing Station (MEPS) for my physical and other testing, and that's what I did.

I went home and told Dad and Mom what I was about to do and that I had to go to MEPS for an initial screening before signing anything, along with them since I was only seventeen. I wasn't allowed to sign an initial inactive reserve contract unless both of my parents consented.

A few weeks later I was at MEPS to go through the entire physical and mental screening and ASVAB testing processes. What a mess that place was, and if you've ever served in the military, you know exactly what I'm talking about. Government inefficiency at its finest, and where every military person first learns the expression "Hurry up and wait!" Nonetheless, everything checked out, and most importantly, I was clean with no sign of drugs in my system.

I was worried something might still be present, but somehow everything was good to go. I think God made sure of it. I also scored well enough on my ASVAB testing to qualify for and be guaranteed an administrative job or Military Occupational Specialty (MOS) group 0100, which is the group of MOS numbers for administrators.

Not long after returning from MEPS, Staff Sergeant Walker came over to our house and talked with Dad and Mom about my planned enlistment before asking them to cosign the initial contract. I couldn't quite get an exact read on either of them in terms of how they were feeling about it, or perhaps it was my own back-and-forth emotions that threw me off.

Dad had this initial look of "Thank God he's doing something to better himself," but then there was also a look of uncertainty. He, too, was probably wondering how in the world I passed the drug test.

Mom was very nervous and seemed afraid and hesitant to sign.

"This is a good option for me, Mom. There's not a lot for me to do here. I'll be in an admin type job, so it'll be fine."

Staff Sergeant Walker gave me a glance, and without saying it again, I knew what he was thinking.

You can die just as easily and at any moment even if you're an admin-type Marine.

I'm sure he didn't say it out loud because this wasn't his first rodeo, and he, too, could sense the fear Mom had. Mom then showed some signs of relief, and I'm sure she was also thinking, *At least he'll have to stop partying and doing drugs.* True, most Marines don't do drugs, or they get kicked out, but they still party.

So in November of 1987, both Dad and Mom signed, and it was official. I was now a poolee, though not yet a Marine.

Chapter 1 of book 2 is titled "The Marines—Basic" because I would not be a Marine until I earned that title in basic training, not just because I signed some stupid contract. Being in the inactive reserves as a poolee means still being a stinking civilian with hopes of eventually getting sent off to basic training or boot camp and eventually earning the title of United States Marine. That said, it was time to get ready.

Much later in my Marine Corps enlistment, Mom told me why she and Dad were hesitant. They genuinely thought I might die, and it was possible, to Staff Sergeant Walker's point. Many a non-infantry Marine have died over the years.

Mom said she cried every day while I was away at basic training and even more after I left for my schooling, first command, and first deployment. However, she said they had been even more afraid of me dying from some sort of drug-related accident or overdose, so that's why they signed.

They also had to endure Donnie's decision to join the Navy, which came not long after I decided to join the Marines. I think he, too, felt he needed to do something, but he didn't want to commit to something like the Marines.

I began to go to monthly poolee meetings at the recruiting station. I had about ten months to get ready mentally and physically.

I started running a little, doing push-ups, pull-ups, and various other calisthenics.

I also kept drinking, smoking a little weed, and occasionally doing other illegal substances when tempted. They didn't drug test you as a poolee, so I knew I wouldn't get caught.

I was trying. I really was, but it's hard to quit cold turkey. That few weeks before going to MEPS to get tested was tough. Ask any recovering addict.

Although I wasn't an alcoholic and I wasn't addicted to any one drug, I was addicted to the general high, so to speak, and the fun of it.

All that said, I got more disciplined with each monthly poolee meeting I went to. I could see how our recruiters were putting in every effort to help us get ready, and I wanted to honor that. A transformation was beginning.

Donnie and I went to see our cousin Stevie graduate from basic training at Marine Corps Recruit Depot in Parris Island, South Carolina, that spring of 1988. We drove down with our uncle Hershel, aunt Maxine, and cousin Tina. It was an awesome experience. Uncle Hershel asked me, "Does seeing these Drill Instructors make you want to change your mind? You think you can handle this?"

"No, it doesn't, and yes, I can handle this."

11
Turning Points: Three

HALFWAY OR MORE THROUGH MY senior year, I realized being a senior was expensive. Pictures, graduation packets, and parties cost money, and Dad and Mom still had no money. So I decided it was time to once again find a job, a legal job and not selling dope.

I hadn't had a real job since my paper route. There were three McDonald's restaurants in Chillicothe at the time, so I thought I should have a good chance of getting on there, perhaps the one on Western Avenue, which was only a mile and a half from our house.

I got hired! Unfortunately, it wasn't for the Western Avenue location. It was for the location on East Main Street, all the way at the very eastern end of town near Highway 23.

Nonetheless, this was turning point number three.

It was nowhere near as significant as the first two turning points, but it was a big step for me. It kept me busy, which also helped keep me disciplined, and it provided a source of legitimate income I had to manage—or try to manage.

My brother-in-law, Don, was the one who drove me to the interview. When I came out and told him I got hired and the location, I asked him if I could live with him and Sally to finish out my senior year. They lived on East Fourth Street, which was less than a mile from the McDonald's where I was hired.

Don said he was cool with that, and he thought Sally would be too. They charged me a little rent to offset the food costs and whatnot. I can't even remember what it was, but my paycheck was able to cover it.

When Don took me home, I walked inside and told Dad and Mom I got a job and was moving out. It was one of those moments I really wish I could have taken back or had a do-over for.

Dad immediately said no. I was still a minor. Mom was just upset. I told Dad I didn't care, I had a job and needed to live closer because we didn't have a car, and there was no way I was riding the city bus that far to get to and from work.

I went upstairs and grabbed my mattress, dragging it down and through the living room. Dad was yelling at me.

Donnie said something to the effect of, "Dude, what the hell are you doing?"

I pushed him and cursed at him, telling him to get out of my way or I would knock him out. It was such a stupid moment for me.

It's a lame excuse, but my strong will was on display, and I was determined to get this job and make some money. Like I said, I wish I could do it over and approach Dad, Mom, and Donnie more calmly.

I'm sorry, Donnie.

I've told him that before, but it's worth repeating. I did tell Dad and Mom sorry later.

Don went to Dad in a much more controlled and polite manner and said, "Hey, maybe he can just come stay with us for a month or so until we can figure something out. He really wants this job and is trying to get his life figured out."

Dad very reluctantly agreed, but I didn't take the mattress. Honestly, I'm not even sure why I grabbed that thing. Don and Sally had a couch I could sleep on.

I'm not sure if I ever told Don thank you for his role in that moment. I did tell him and Sally thanks multiple times for letting me live with them, but Don was good to me and ended up driving me to and from work a lot.

So I was off. Mom continued crying as I was leaving. She knew I'd eventually move out of the house for good. I had to go, though, as I was starting work that Monday evening after school.

Living with Sally and Don worked out fine. They gave me a fair amount of freedom, but they also had some rules of when to be home, etc. It didn't matter because I was busy working. I took five-to-ten p.m. shifts, and on the weekends, I worked full eight-hour shifts. Between that and school, since I was studying again, I didn't have a lot of time on my hands for the usual shenanigans.

A couple of months later, Dad and Mom moved back down to the east end. For the first time, it wasn't about them getting evicted. They really wanted me back in the house to finish up my senior year and to spend the summer with them before I left for basic training that fall.

They rented a house on Adams Street, which wasn't far from Don and Sally and within walking distance of McDonald's. They also gave me a room in the basement, which was cool. There was a bench press and some weights the previous tenants had left, so I was able to lift a little to improve my strength and conditioning.

So, after moving back in with Dad and Mom, things seemed to be going well. I continued with my poolee meetings and was getting in better shape. Between that, school, and work, I also slowed down on the hard-core partying quite a bit but was still having a great time as a senior. Another good turning point.

12
Turning Points: Four

IT SEEMED LIKE I WAS on cruise control when one day at school Becky approached me.

"I want you to know I'm pregnant. It's your baby."

Wait, what?

I didn't say that out loud, but it's what went through my head.

I immediately reminded her that she started seeing other guys after we broke up, and another blond-hair, blue-eyed guy in particular. At the same time, I also remembered that we had hooked up the past December, but I chose to ignore that fact. Her first trimester pregnancy lined up well with this timing. She insisted it was my baby, but I honestly wasn't sure.

I guess I did what most seventeen-year-old boys do who find out they've possibly gotten a girl pregnant. I had a stupid, initial reaction. It was likely out of fear, the unknown, or the demons that still lingered around me as I was trying to take a different path.

"Get an abortion."

"I'm not going to do that. I'm having this baby."

"Whatever! You'll have to get a test to make sure it's mine."

I walked away and just ignored her the rest of the school year and all summer long after graduating.

I was constantly reminded of her pregnancy by passing her in the school hallways and seeing her belly growing throughout the remainder of the school year, but I left her to deal with it on her own.

This was turning point number four.

Unfortunately, this was a bad turning point because of how I dealt with it. However, it eventually became one of the most important turning points of my life.

The right thing to have done, even if I wasn't sure the baby was mine but on the very good chance it was, would have been to at least try to help. I was working, so I could have given her some money for doctor bills, rides to the doctor, or anything else she might have needed.

I didn't. I was selfish, and I was determined to stay focused on graduating, getting ready for the Marines, and hanging out with friends as much as possible before leaving.

I'm sorry, Becky.

I don't think I have ever apologized for that selfish young boy who left you all to yourself at age sixteen to deal with a pregnancy. I know it was a long time ago, but I'm sorry. I can't imagine what it must have been like to be a very young single mother.

Before we knew it, in early June 1988, Donnie and I graduated together from Chillicothe High School!

We had a huge gathering of family in attendance, who cheered loudly as they first called Donnie's name and then mine. We did it, and it felt good to walk across the stage with my brother. We went out and partied all night long and at least for a couple of days. We had a great time. However, Donnie was set to leave for the Navy the very next week. He wouldn't get to enjoy the summer like I was planning to do.

It was midweek following the weekend we graduated when Donnie had to leave. Since school was out, I had agreed to work a full eight-hour shift at McDonald's.

Both Donnie and I were up already, and after I got dressed and was about to leave, I said to him, "All right, man. Good luck to you. You're gonna do great. I'll see you later, man. I need to get to work."

I think I might have given him a sort of sideways man hug, and that was it.

Later that day around four p.m., I got off work and walked home. I came through the front door and said, "Mom?" Yep, always the first person I asked for.

"I'm in here, honey."

"How's it going? Did the recruiters come and get Donnie? Is everything good?"

Donnie was quiet that morning. Not his usual self, for sure. So I was genuinely concerned he was going to be all right.

"He didn't go, honey."

"What, really? What happened? Where is he?"

"He changed his mind. The recruiters were upset, but I guess there's nothing they can do as he only signed the initial agreement. I guess he's supposed to swear in a second time before they can make him go. He went down to the park to play basketball."

I immediately went to go find Donnie. I knew he was probably embarrassed about not going. I found him shooting hoops with some other guys.

"Hey, man, what's going on? Mom told me what happened. Hey, it's your choice what you want to do, so no big deal. Now we have all summer to party."

"Thanks, man," was all he said, and we did indeed go partying that night. I guess to celebrate him continuing as a civilian.

Donnie's decision did not affect my decision. I was still as determined as ever to join the Marines.

That said, Donnie and I drank practically every night that summer of 1988, as I was primarily working day shifts at McDonald's and he hadn't started working yet. We went to the east end, west end, and any other end where there was a party. My eighteenth birthday was off the charts partying, along with so many others who were also turning eighteen that summer. It was a great summer and a real time of bonding for Donnie and me.

I will never forget that summer; I wanted to have as great a time as possible before heading out in September, and that's what we did.

For good measure, and I can't quite remember exactly why this time, we ended up moving about a mile from Adams Street to Fourth Street later that summer. It was such a blur and not nearly as significant as some of the other moves we had made over the years. For me, it was my last move with Dad and Mom. Donnie shared with me later they ended up moving about four more times during my first year of being in the Marines.

That might have driven me crazy, but I guess Donnie just rolled with it until he could work enough to move out on his own someday.

Just like that, in the blink of an eye, as they say, my life with Dad, Mom, and all my siblings was ending. I was about to embark on a whole new chapter of life. One I really had no idea where it would take me. I just knew at that time, I was done with all that had happened from my first memories there in Chillicothe and up to this point.

Yes, I would really miss Mom, and yes, I would really miss Donnie, whom I had gotten so close with again over the last year and a half. However, I was ready, and my ship date for the Marines was fast approaching.

There was one last temptation of sorts when the manager of the McDonald's I worked at asked me to stay. He said he could make me a junior manager, and he talked about how good the bonuses were once you made the manager position. He said it with as serious a face and tone I'd ever heard. Perhaps he saw something in me that made him make such an offer. Some drive and determination. I'm not sure, but I was flattered.

I told him I really appreciated the offer, and I really enjoyed my time at McDonald's. It had helped me through a major transitional phase in my life, to grow up and mature a bit. Then, after a pause, I said something to the effect that I still needed more discipline and structure in my life, and I had already committed to joining the United States Marine Corp. I was determined to become a Marine.

I worked at McDonald's through the summer and up until just a couple of weeks before it was time to ship out. I was ready. Let's go!

13
Brice:
The Baby and Young Boy

JUST AS I WAS SAYING, "Let's go!" Becky's doctor was likely saying something very similar. You see, my son, Brice, was born three days before I was supposed to ship out to Parris Island, South Carolina, for Marine Corps basic training.

When I told Brice I was going to write a book and it would include him, he gave me one bit of advice. "Just be honest, Dad. Be totally honest regardless of the cost."

That's what I intend to do, out of respect for Brice and because I want to uphold my current reputation of integrity. Yeah, I had very little when I was younger.

As I mentioned in chapter 12, I wasn't around for Becky's pregnancy. I also wasn't there when Brice was born. I'm sorry, Becky and Brice.

Becky came to our house the day she got out of the hospital. It must have been a day or two before I was to be picked up by the recruiters and shipped out, which was September 11. She wanted to show me the baby, and she knew Mom would adore that baby.

I was in my bedroom. I had just woken up after one final night partying, so I was a little groggy. Aside from that, all I had on my mind was that I was about to ship out very soon.

Yes, this is my way of hopefully softening the blow of sharing my next actions.

Becky knocked on the door and asked to come in. I sat up and told her to come in. She was carrying the baby and, with a huge smile and full of pride, said, "I want to show you our son."

I took one look at that baby and literally thought, and I believe even said out loud, "That's not my kid."

I'm sorry, Becky and Brice.

His hair was dark, nearly black, and his skin was a reddish, purplish color. I was as blond as they come with blue eyes, and Becky had lighter hair too, and both of us were as white as can be.

Without saying it, my theory of her perhaps getting pregnant from the other blond-haired, blue-eyed boy she dated after me was dispelled quickly as I ran different theories and scenarios through my head. She must have gotten pregnant from some other dude, I thought.

I was an eighteen-year-old punk kid trying to turn into a decent young man, but I didn't know the first thing about babies.

Many are born with darker hair that turns lighter, and almost all babies have that reddish, purple skin at first. But I went with my theory to deny Brice was my son.

I repeated what I told her when she revealed her pregnancy, that we needed to get a paternity test done.

"He's your son!" she insisted, as one would expect her to since she was bringing him to my house to introduce him.

"Well, prove it. We can have a test done when I get back from boot camp."

Becky left quick after, and that was it for the moment.

After she left, Mom instantly said to me, "That's your baby, honey. He looks like you."

"That kid is not mine, Mom. She was messing around with all kinds of other guys."

Of course, I really didn't know who Becky had been with, and I only knew of the one boy. However, I was having none of that. My strong will persisted as I prepared to leave.

That said, I couldn't shake the reality a baby had been born, and I was claimed to be the father. My type A personality had to know for sure, so I kept saying to myself, *We'll just get a test done as soon as we can.*

Just as my strong will persisted, Mom's strong will also persisted. It's funny how moms just know certain things. Becky fits in that category too.

Mom said, "Well, I'll keep an eye on her and the baby while you're away."

"All right, Mom. Whatever."

She did. I'm not exactly sure how often Becky came around, but I suspect it was often. I wrote a lot of letters to Dad, Mom, Donnie, and sometimes the girls. Mom always wrote back, "I hope you're doing okay there, honey. Becky and the baby are doing fine. He's getting big. He looks like you."

During my first Marine Corps enlistment, I didn't come home all that often. Ten days after boot camp. Just a few days after my MOS school. A few days in the late summer of 1989 before my first eight-month deployment. Maybe ten days after my first deployment when I bought my first car. Then a second deployment of ten months only seven months after returning from my first one due to the Gulf War.

When I got home from my second deployment, it was October 1991. Just like that, Brice was three years old.

I missed all three of those birthdays, with the first and third being deployed in Japan, and the second just doing my thing stationed in North Carolina. I don't recall seeing Brice at all those first three years, other than pictures Mom sent, around his birthday, at Christmas, and other holidays.

I'm sorry, Brice.

I do know Becky and Brice ended up living with Dad and Mom for some time during that three-year period. At least someone in our family was doing their part.

In November 1991, I came home on leave after my second deployment. Before coming up to Ohio on leave, someone had suggested to me I should try to be more involved in Brice's life and to perhaps give it another try with Becky. So I thought I would.

One day, Becky had left Brice at the house for some reason. Mom was being, well, Mom and continued to insist Brice was my son.

He was sleeping at the time, so I just sort of looked at him for a little while and gave it some thought. His hair was lighter than the last time I saw him in person. That was a start.

He woke up a little, so I tried to bond with him. We've all seen those commercials or advertisements where a dad has their baby or toddler lying on their chest, both asleep. Well, that's what I tried to do for a moment. However, Brice looked at me like, *Who the heck is this guy?* so that didn't go as planned. Mom to the rescue because he knew her well. Thanks, Mom.

I did try to reconnect with Becky, and of course that involved hooking up again. It lasted for a few days while I was home on leave. I did interact a little more with Brice when at her house, and he warmed up some. Honestly, I think I was still very much a stranger to him. Maybe he had seen pictures of me from Mom, but that's not the same.

For as hard as I thought I tried, I couldn't reconnect with Becky. Maybe I didn't try hard enough. I just felt annoyed with her, like she had interrupted my life and inserted herself into my family. She surely had Mom convinced.

I brought up the paternity test, and she basically said we didn't need to have it done. That only annoyed me further and made me even more skeptical. I began to wonder, *What if I start investing time with her and Brice and he's not even my son?* So once again, I walked away from them and headed back down to North Carolina after my leave.

Life went on. I missed Brice's fourth birthday in 1992. I was passing through Ohio on my way to California that September of 1992. However, I was more focused on "Gotta go see about a girl" because during that year, I had fallen in love with another girl who lived out there.

Yes, that "girl" was my beautiful wife, Kahala.

I only stayed in Ohio a few days, and in my mind, I had no time to waste on Becky if she wasn't ready to take a paternity test.

Fast-forward not too far into the fall of 1993. Becky was receiving welfare and food stamps for her and Brice. I'm not sure what triggered it in Ohio or if it was a federal requirement, but the state of Ohio told Becky that for her to continue receiving welfare and food stamps, she had to name a father for Brice. Of course, she named me, which then triggered the state of Ohio to demand of me a paternity test.

After five years of asking for a paternity test Becky didn't grant, the state of Ohio granted it. Finally.

For the first time in five years, the possibility of being a dad really set in. I was nervous. I was ordered to go to a nearby lab in Los Angeles, where I lived at the time, and have a buccal swab done. It was then sent off to another lab that specialized in genetic marker testing. After about three to four weeks, I received a letter in the mail with a carbon copy also going to the state of Ohio.

The letter confirmed Brice was indeed my son! The letter showed a very high percentage of accuracy, which made it undeniable.

There it was in black and white. Finally, I knew for sure and could stop wondering.

After that, all the "I told you so" comments came in. Surely from Becky and Mom, although Mom's was more like "I knew he was your son, honey. I could just tell."

Mom was way gentler with the news. The others who said he was my son were more peanut gallery, to which I replied, "And yes, I've been asking to find out for the last five years."

They of course ignored that part and looked to cast judgment.

At this point I was five years in with the Marine Corps, on my second enlistment, and way more mature than I was in 1988. My personality type, and my strong inner desire to make things right made me want to act quickly toward being a dad.

The state of Ohio also acted quickly and, through some administrative proceeding, suggested an inordinately high child support amount so they could then reduce their welfare and food stamp support. I can't quite remember the number they proposed, but it would have left me unable to afford my apartment, car payment, and you name it. It was a crazy monthly amount. They also suggested a back pay amount that was just as ridiculous.

I hired a child custody attorney, whose name I can't remember, but she was good. Due to my military status, she argued and received judgment that I didn't even have to appear in person at the administrative proceedings. She was able to act on my behalf.

Due to my written testimony, I had requested a paternity test from the point of first finding out Becky was pregnant, and apparently Becky didn't deny it, my attorney was able to get the back pay child support waived.

She also successfully argued the amount being requested by the state of Ohio was unreasonable, showing them my Leave and Earnings Statements from the Marines as proof I didn't have enough money to live on in the Los Angeles area. They lowered the monthly amount being requested by hundreds of dollars.

I said she was good, but she was almost too good. The monthly amount was something like $250 a month, which really seemed too little. When I asked her about it, she strongly advised me to let it go, and if I wanted to pay more on my own, I could. However, she also strongly advised me against that, saying Becky could take us back to court and make it mandatory.

So I only paid the $250 a month. When Brice came to visit, I made up for it by trying my best to do as many fun things as possible.

In December of 1993, after the child support was established but before there were any legal custody rights established, Kahala and I were back in Ohio for Christmas. Becky had agreed to let Brice stay with us during Christmas Eve and Christmas Day. We were staying at Donna's house.

We were enjoying our time together and trying to bond as much as possible. However, Becky had spoken with Sally and gotten all riled up about something. She called and said she changed her mind and no longer felt comfortable having Brice stay with me. She wouldn't specify as to why, which was totally lame.

I told her this was ridiculous and I had a right to see him, especially since I was now paying child support. She quickly said there was no official custody papers, and she was coming to get him.

Hoping she was bluffing, we had already laid down for the night. Again, it was Christmas Eve. Sure enough, there was a knock at the door. I answered it, and it was Becky with her then husband and her sister as well. It was snowing outside, so we let her in, only to have her arguing with me in front of Brice. Her sister also decided to pull Kahala to the side and start trying to create drama there, suggesting there was still something to my relationship with Becky. Not true, of course.

Here it was Christmas Eve, and she was tearing him away from us late at night, and for what? Just to prove that she could since there were no custody papers.

So she took him, and there wasn't anything I could do. She threatened to call the cops if I didn't let him go. Suddenly, I wasn't so upset about her not getting as much money each month, but honestly, in the end, it only hurt Brice.

I guess I was naive enough to think Becky would just allow me to see Brice since I was paying child support. I was hoping to avoid going back to court for the custody part. I really couldn't afford it. However, this straw quickly broke the camel's back. As soon as we got back to California, I called my attorney, and she went to work on getting noncustodial parental rights established.

In just a couple of months, the noncustodial parent custody rights were established. I was allowed to have Brice for six weeks each summer and on alternating holidays if I was in Ohio. I was also allowed to call him whenever I wanted, which I reserved mostly for the weekends.

In the summer of 1994, Mom accompanied Brice to Huntington Beach, California, where we were living at the time. Becky had no choice but to let him come. However, she called frequently. I can understand a mom wanting to talk to her child, but this wasn't her motivation.

Becky knew we wanted to spend as much enjoyable time as possible with Brice when he was visiting. In fact, we hit all the various amusement parks and other local attractions over the next six-plus years living in California between Huntington Beach and then Oceanside.

We went to Disneyland, Knott's Berry Farm, the Long Beach Aquarium, deep-sea fishing, and you name it. When we lived in Oceanside, we became members of the world-famous San Diego Zoo, the San Diego Wild Animal Park (now called the San Diego Zoo Safari Park), and Sea World, so we frequented those locations as well. Of course, there was always some beach time.

I took as much leave as possible, but eventually I had to work over the course of the six weeks. Kahala then entertained Brice as much as she could by taking time off from her work, if she was working at the time.

I like to think that Brice had a really good time when he visited as a kid and young teenager. He smiled and laughed a lot when we were together. However, I'm convinced Becky didn't want that to happen. She was too afraid of him possibly wanting to come live with us. Just like she was too afraid of taking a paternity test for five years, she was now afraid of losing her custodial parental rights should he start suggesting he'd rather live with us.

Whenever Becky called him during our visits, her motivation was to convince Brice life was better with her. She promised him the world . . . "as soon as you get home."

Brice later told me her promises were empty nearly 100 percent of the time. It was usually promises of elaborate gifts that she didn't buy. Unfortunately, the pattern repeated itself every time he was with us.

It's sad parents can't simply be happy their kid is happy, regardless of whose custody they're in. It would make kids' lives much easier if parents weren't so selfish. It would also make hard times and tragic events much easier to deal with, and as we know, those are inevitable in life.

14
Brice:
The Hard Years

IN 1997, RIGHT AFTER BRICE'S birthday, Brice and Becky were both severely burned by a grease fire in their kitchen. Brice had to have multiple skin grafts done to treat his burns. Once I found out, I immediately went back to see him at Children's Hospital in Columbus.

I tried to focus on Brice and stayed there in Ohio until he was out of critical condition. I did not go to visit Becky. She ended up getting out of the hospital much sooner than Brice, so I did see her. She looked bad, but there was no love lost between us at this point, especially with all the games she played when he was in my custody or whenever I tried to call.

Although scarred, Brice recovered from his burns, and life went on. We had calls, summer visits, and visits over holidays when we were back in Ohio. Although it was pretty much the same with Becky, I learned to tune her out and told myself someday Brice will grow up and realize the difference.

He did.

I never once talked bad about her to Brice. I'm not convinced she extended me the same courtesy. However, at one point a few years after the fire, Becky suggested the possibility of him coming to live with me. I was shocked. Considering there was zero trust between us, and after having been mistreated by her multiple times before, I felt this was a trap. So I told her I wasn't sure about it and wanted to give it some thought. I'm not sure what was going on in her life at that time or if she was sincere or not, but it didn't come up again.

Becky divorced her husband, Brice's sister's dad, and she eventually moved in with another guy named Dan. He was there during some of Brice's more formative years.

Brice tells me he was a good guy, and he showed Brice how to do a lot of things related to construction. I'm grateful for that. However, the one thing I never did approve of was Becky insisting Brice call him Dad. That really annoyed me.

I was also annoyed at Dan for even allowing it. Who the hell did he think he was? I could see if maybe he had married Becky and they were trying to make a family, but these two never got married. They only shacked up, and then he eventually left her.

I don't blame Brice. What did he know? I know Brice still holds him in high regard because he was there way more than I was, but he is not his dad. I am.

In 2006, as Brice was nearing high school graduation, he was considering a variety of different options after high school. We talked about it quite a bit at his graduation party we held for him at Donnie's house.

He liked to cook, especially a good steak, so he was thinking of going to a culinary school in Ohio. I told him I thought that was a great idea and, regardless of his decision, I would support him.

However, I also think Brice was trying to make a deeper connection with me. Perhaps it was because Kahala and I had Malia and Micah at that time. Perhaps it was because of the Dan situation. Or perhaps it was because we didn't fully connect while he was growing up due to our whole noncustodial parent arrangement. As hard as we tried, we only got to see each other a couple of times a year.

Eventually Brice decided to join the United States Marine Corps. He followed in my footsteps, although I wasn't convinced that was really his first or most sincere choice. Nonetheless, I thought it was a great opportunity for him.

Brice left for basic training on September 10, and his official join date was September 11, 2006. In three short months (not really), he was graduating as a United States Marine!

I very much remember going to Brice's graduation from basic training. It was the first time being back at Parris Island since 1988, eighteen years later in December 2006. I thought it was cool Brice left in September and graduated in December like I did.

Aside from the awkwardness of his mom being there at graduation, having an even more awkward breakfast with her and his little sister, who kept opening and eating multiple sugar packets, along with his incredibly shy girlfriend, now wife, Shannon, who joined us but hardly spoke, it was a very proud moment spending a family day with him and watching him graduate. Even though I was now a veteran five years in the making, I thought for sure this would help us connect further.

I was wrong.

After Brice graduated from basic training, he eventually went to Mass Communications school at Ft. Meade near Baltimore, Maryland, where he learned to be a combat cameraman. He was in school for about six months, and in June 2007, he got stationed at Marine Corps Air Station in Yuma, Arizona.

Of course, I was following along through occasional phone calls during this entire time. However, sometime in early 2008, Donnie called me and said there was a notice and picture of Brice and Shannon in the local newspaper indicating they had gotten married. I thought it must have been a mistake and didn't want to believe it. I was embarrassed he found out before I did.

I called Brice immediately to ask about it. He confirmed it was true.

"Oh wow! Did that just happen? Did you guys sort of elope like Kahala and I did?"

"No, we got married after boot camp, back in January 2007."

That was a punch in the gut. He had been married a year and didn't tell me.

"Why didn't you let me know?"

"I didn't think you would approve."

"It really doesn't matter to me. I just wish I'd known."

"Well, there's something else too. She's pregnant and the baby is due in June."

Another punch in the gut, although that one wasn't as upsetting.

"Okay, wow! That's great. Maybe we can come down and visit when the baby is born."

"Sure, that'd be fine."

We eventually hung up, but I was pretty taken aback by this call. I kept wondering why he didn't tell me. What was the real reason? Did he think I was too judgmental and didn't want me to pass judgment about his marriage?

Shannon seemed like a nice girl, quiet but nice, and very smart and pretty, so I thought she would make a wonderful wife for Brice. It would have been nice to have known about it. Maybe we could have helped them in some way.

But why didn't he tell me? Maybe it was the lack of connection, a lack of trust, or again, maybe he thought I would judge him? Had I judged him before? Maybe. Would it be the last time? No, unfortunately not.

Brice told me later he wanted to get married before going to his combat cameraman school in order to get benefits for being married. He also told me his mom didn't think I should know, and she supported him not telling me.

Now, at this point Brice was eighteen, a United States Marine, and could own his decisions. However, I was very angry with Becky. I would never in a thousand years keep something like that from another parent. It's just wrong. She should have done the right thing and not been so selfish.

Shortly after my granddaughter Scarlet was born in June 2008, we went down to MCAS Yuma to visit. It was a little awkward at first, but we put that aside and enjoyed the visit with my first granddaughter. She was adorable and still is to this day.

Brice and Shannon went on to have another daughter, Sara, nearly two years later in May 2010. She, too, was and still is adorable. Brice had a cute little family, and I was very happy for them.

In spring of 2010, Brice got orders to Marine Corps Base Camp Pendleton, California. He only had a little over a year left, but they made him transfer. He ended up sending Shannon and the girls back to Ohio since his intentions were to leave the Marine Corps after his current enlistment.

They stopped and saw us on their way back to Ohio as we were living in Wichita, Kansas, at the time. It was a nice visit, but they were eventually off. They had bought a house in Logan, Ohio, and Brice needed to get them settled there before heading back to Camp Pendleton.

Shortly after Brice got to Camp Pendleton in June 2010, he called and told me he was being deployed to Afghanistan in October with the Second Battalion, First Marines infantry unit. He sounded scared. Hell, who wouldn't be a little frightened of the thought of going into that situation? So many Marines and others were being killed daily. I tried to reassure him and suggested he pray for God's protection and the same for Shannon and the girls while he was away, as we were praying as well. Thankfully, he suffered no physical harm while there for about eight months.

When Brice got home from Afghanistan in May 2011, I spoke with him and asked if he might reconsider reenlisting and staying in the Marines. He was about to attain the rank of Sergeant, which is a very respectable rank. He said no, he wanted to get out and move back to Ohio. I asked him what he was going to do, but he wasn't sure.

I told him I could possibly help him get a photography business going since he was well trained in that and was very good at it as well. He said maybe, but I didn't get the sense he wanted any help. I'm not sure why. He seemed very indecisive. Something wasn't right.

Brice eventually got promoted to Sergeant, but he still got out of the Marine Corps in September 2011 after serving five years, and he went home. We didn't talk all that much initially after he got out. I thought he was busy readjusting back to civilian life and getting things figured out. We were also in the process of selling our home in Wichita and moving to Colorado.

However, sometime before we moved, around early November of 2011, Brice and I had one final phone call that year and what would be for the next ten months.

I called Brice after he'd just posted a picture of himself with Scarlet and Sara on Facebook, and he had his ears pierced. I was thinking of his transition and potential job opportunities, but for some reason something prompted me to say the stupidest thing.

I told Brice that he would have to explain his piercings and tattoos to Malia and Micah when they saw him. I said they'll wonder what they are and what they're all about. Brice promptly said, "I don't have to explain myself to anyone."

He was right, but in a bullheaded moment, I kept arguing with him about it. Frankly, it was one of my worst, most judgmental moments ever.

Who the hell did I think I was, and what right did I have making that sort of statement? I don't know what I was thinking.

Brice said he had to go and hung up the phone. So I went on Facebook to further the conversation. I just couldn't help myself.

He blocked me. Shannon blocked me. The feud was on. Maybe that was why Brice didn't tell me about him getting married? Maybe I was too judgmental, another typical judgmental Christian?

Saint Teresa of Calcutta once said, "If you judge people, you have no time to love them." She was and still is right.

Once we had moved to Colorado, I realized just how awful that moment was, and after even deeper self-reflection, I also realized I had somehow become a judgmental Christian.

Over the course of the next six to nine months, I texted Brice every now and then saying I was sorry. He didn't answer.

It wasn't until September 8, 2012, when I texted him on his birthday to say happy birthday and once again say I'm sorry, that he finally called.

I was finally able to tell him I'm sorry in person, or at least voice to voice. I also told him how losing him for nearly a year was painful. What I didn't realize is how much pain and suffering Brice had endured during that same time.

I won't go into detail, but after serving in Afghanistan, then getting out of the Marines during this time we weren't talking, and especially as a Sergeant where you really can be considered on top of the world in the military, he had hit rock bottom. He was in a downward spiral when we had our blowup. I only accelerated it.

Over the course of us recovering our relationship, because it didn't happen in just that one phone call, I felt that we were bonding and sharing more and more. Like I said, I honestly think the estrangement was more my fault than Brice's. I felt I had finally removed the blinders I was wearing, the self-righteous Christian blinders. I was no longer judging like I had somehow learned to do over the course of many years as a Christian.

I learned to listen, and Brice had a lot to say. He still has a lot to say today, as do I, and I feel we are now closer than ever. He's a better listener and is patient with me when I ramble on the phone.

For as bad as those ten months or so were, God can bring good from such circumstances. That time helped me to be a better person, a better Christian, and I'm thankful Brice gave me another chance to prove it. Although I'm not and will never be perfect, I'm trying and doing better than before that time.

Thank you, Brice.

To say that I'm proud of Brice today is an understatement. He has now given us four beautiful granddaughters with the addition of "the littles," the youngest two girls, named Sophia and Sable. They're adorable. I try to visit with them at least twice a year.

Brice and Shannon have created a beautiful home. He's working hard in the trades as an insulator and is well respected by the company he works for. He's also a veteran and Marine for life, so that, too, gives us a lot to talk about.

I hope and pray you are not estranged from a child or a parent. I know forgiveness can be hard sometimes, depending on the circumstances. If possible, I encourage you to try to forgive. You may even have to forgive a few times to get through the process.

I also fully understand you might have forgiven but cannot subject yourself to further potential abuse, whether it be physical, mental, or emotional. However, if there's even the most remote chance they could do better, maybe give it a try. I'm incredibly grateful Brice made the choice to give me another chance.

Thank you, bud. I love you, and I hope to only further strengthen our relationship.

In case anyone is wondering, I clearly had some harsh words for Becky in the last two chapters. Although we still don't talk much, I hold no ill will toward her whatsoever. I have completely forgiven her, and I hope she has or will do the same for me. I only wish she and her current husband the best, and I know she, too, only wants the best for Brice and his family.

I realize these last two chapters strayed from the chronological order of events I was sharing and went fast-forward through much of Brice's life. However, I felt it important to share these stories given their significance and since Brice entered my life before the Marines.

With that, let's talk about the Marines! Let's go!

Epilogue

YOU NOW HAVE SOME INSIGHTS about my childhood and teenage years. Hate, love, prayer, dysfunction, drugs, turning points, bad decisions, and then some good decisions, and new life. Glimmers of hope.

Nonetheless, a foundation was laid, far from perfect and shaped by so many life-altering and challenging events. Yet it would all prepare me for what was to come over the course of the next thirteen years, the Marine years. Many more life-altering and challenging events, but also more hope, in a far different world than South Central Ohio.

I hope you will continue the journey with me.

About the Author

RONALD LEE SPARKS WAS BORN in Circleville, Ohio, and raised in Chillicothe, Ohio. He currently resides in Colorado. The Yellow House series is an autobiography of his most influential life experiences that helped shape and define who he is today.

The Yellow House: Foundations, or book one of Sparks's three-book series, shares stories of growing up in South Central Ohio and experiencing incredibly personal and family-related struggle and pain. It resulted in him becoming a lost and deeply troubled teen who ventured into deep, dark waters, seemingly to the point of no return, before eventually finding an escape path.

The stories and events he shares, some significant and some less so by worldly standards, along with real people, made up of family, friends, and adversaries, are believed to have been placed in his path as part of God's plan. He admits it's hard to see the plan in book one, and most of the stories and events were likely not God's will, but they were still part of a plan for eventual good and prosperity in Sparks's life.

Some of the stories, events, and experiences shared may have triggered strong emotions, feelings, and unwanted thoughts. The intention of this book, however, was to share the author's life experiences and belief that regardless of where you start in life, or what life throws at you along the way, there is always hope and good that can come from it.